A Tasteful Century

A Tasteful Century

Forsyth County Public Library
1906-2006

Forsyth County
Public Library

Celebrate a Century!

Winston-Salem, North Carolina
www.forsythlibrary.org

Published by John F. Blair, Publisher
Winston-Salem, North Carolina

The paper in this book meets the guidelines for permanence and durability of the Committee on Production Guidelines for Book Longevity of the Council on Library Resources.

Design by Angela Harwood
Photograph of Carnegie Library circa 1906 courtesy of the
Forsyth County Public Library Photograph Collection
Cover Photograph by Rob Norwood

Library of Congress Cataloging-in-Publication Data

A tasteful century : Forsyth County Public Library 1906-2006 / edited by Forsyth County Library.
p. cm.
ISBN-13: 978-0-89587-344-6 (alk. paper)
ISBN-10: 0-89587-344-3 (alk. paper)
1. Cookery, American. I. Forsyth County Public Library.

TX715.T2148 2006
641.5'973—dc22
2006028429

CONTENTS

Foreword ix
For the Library xi
The Twin-City Housewife xiii
Notes to This Volume xv

RECIPES

✾ *indicates that recipe is from* Favorite Recipes: Forsyth County Public Library Staff 1976

APPETIZERS 1

Baked Onion Dip—Teresa Floyd 2
Black Bean Hummus—Ben Morgan 2
Bonnie's Clam Dip—Bonnie Fulp 2
Spinach Artichoke Dip—Kathleen Wheeless 3
Julie's Guacamole—Julie Walker 3
Dip for Tortilla Chips—Judy Prater 4
Easy Mexican Dip—Judy Fishel Joyce 4
Layered Taco Dip—Jennifer Wiseman 4
Margot Wharton's Tex-Mex Dip—Margot Wharton 5
Joy White's Spinach Spread—Joy White 5
Blue Cheese Ball ✾—Marty Reith 6
Spicy Cheese Log—Carole Bonnell 6
Pepperoni Cheese Ball—Jennifer Wiseman 6
Salmon Ball—Barbara Anderson 7
Cheese Krispies—Sharon Watts 7
Cheese Pennies ✾—Anne Correll 8
Crabbies—Lise Keppler 8
Spinach Tortilla Roll-Ups—Sandy Dwyer 9
Asparagus Rolls ✾—Diane Burrows 9
Sweet and Sour Avocados—Dolores Sampedro 10
Bob Rickert's Shrimp Cocktail Sauce—Bob Rickert 10

SALADS 11

Broad Bean Salad (Fool Midammis) ✾—Aleya El Maghrabi 12
Calico Salad ✾—Louise Pulley 12
Marinated Cucumber Salad—Julie James 13
Marinated Cabbage Slaw—Karen Robertson 13
Marinated Tomatoes—Yolanda Pickett 14
Copper Pennies—Jessica and Gail Cole 14
French Dressing—Jessica and Gail Cole 14
Tossed Salad with Fruit and Nuts—Carolyn Price 15
Basic Vinaigrette—Carolyn Price 15
Very Berry Spinach Salad—Jessica Cole 15
Raspberry Vinaigrette—Jessica Cole 16
Seven-Layer Salad—Lara Luck 16
24-Hour Salad—Jessica and Gail Cole 17
Low-Fat Potato Salad—DeLois Cue 17
Red-Skin Potato Salad—Sharon Watts 18
South of the Border Potato Salad—Donna L. Staley 18
Orzo and Corn Off the Cob Salad—Betty Allegrone 19
Jell-O® Salad—Sharon Watts 19
Joyce's Cranberry Salad—Jennifer Wiseman 20
Ambrosia—Merrikay Brown 20
Mother Blount's Fantastic Ambrosia—Mitzi Loflin Sapp 21
Jessica's Fruit Salad—Jessica Cole 21
Orange Fruit Salad—Jennifer Wiseman 22
Pineapple Delight—Yvonne Rhodes 22
Black Bean Salsa—Janelle Kent 23
Fennel Seed Vinaigrette—Rob Norwood 23
Burgundy Bacon Vinaigrette—Barbara Rickert 24
Poppy Seed Salad Dressing—Anonymous 24

MAIN COURSES 25

African Chicken and Rice—Pat Stepney 26
Barbecued Chicken—Donna L. Staley 27
Citrus Grilled Chicken—Carole Bonnell 27
Miss Annie's Baked Chicken and Gravy—Annie Johnson 28
Emily Williams's Swiss Chicken Casserole—Emily Williams 28
Jazzed Up Chicken—Ruth Oregar 29
Karen's Mexican Chicken—Karen Robertson 29
Chicken Crescents—Teresa Floyd 30
Texas Chicken Loaf—Charlene Davis 30
Healthy Chicken Salad—Joan Burton 31
Lemon Blueberry Chicken Salad—Donna L. Staley 31
Hot Chicken Salad—Alison Coward 32
Rosemary Pork with Pears—Betty Allegrone 32
Eastern Carolina Barbecue, the Cheater's Version—Lise Keppler 33
Chopped South Carolina Barbecue—Dot Jordan 33
Plantation Casserole ☘—Sylvia Hauser Thompson 34
Down Home Ham and Potato Casserole—Brenda McCloud 34
Jennifer's Meatloaf—Jennifer Wiseman 35
Decca's Combined Family Meatloaf—Decca Riedel 35
Sweet and Sour Meatballs—Lois Willard 36
Carmola Quick Spaghetti—Allison Carmola 36
Barrett Family Spaghetti and Meatballs—Jenny Barrett 37
Robert's Lasagna—Robert Burgin 38
Johnny Brazili—Barbara Rickert 38
Asian Salmon—Mary McAfee 39
Shrimp Jambalaya—Elizabeth Skinner 39
Stir-Fried Shrimp and Snow Peas—Betty Allegrone 40
Georgia Shrimp Bake—Julie Walker 40
Seven Seas Casserole ☘—Elizabeth Hull 41
Spicy Tuna Croquettes—Rhonda B. Scales 41
Barrett Family Macaroni and Cheese—Jenny Barrett 42
Homestyle Four-Cheese Macaroni—Yolanda Bolden 42
Noodles and Broccoli with Saffron—Andrea Morgan 43
Herbed Lentils and Rice—Lise Keppler 44
Three-Pepper Linguini—Betty Allegrone 44
Stuffed Peppers ☘—Nancy Belchee 45
Roasted Beans with Garlic and Olives—Andrea Morgan 46

SOUPS & STEWS 47

Best Ever Crock-Pot® Stew—Dianne Riedel 48
Five-Hour Stew ☘—Bob May 49
Brunswick Stew—Jerry Carroll 49
Chicken Stew—Paul Kwiatkowski 50
Spicy Chili—Art Weeks 50
Vegetarian Chili, Cincinnati Style—Julie James 51
Eggplant Supper Soup—William Durham 52
Mom's Chicken Noodle Soup—Elizabeth Skinner 52
Homemade Vegetable Beef Soup—Teresa Floyd 53
Armenian Lentil Soup—Julie James 53
Curried Pea Soup—Lise Keppler 54
Potato Cheese Soup—Rob Norwood 55
Tuna Chowder—Rob Norwood 55

SIDE DISHES 57

Broccoli Casserole—Judy Prater 58
Broccoli Cheese Casserole—Rob Norwood 58
Broccoli Rice Casserole—Decca Riedel 59
Green Bean Casserole—Teresa Floyd 59
Cheesy Mushroom Green Bean Casserole—Decca Riedel 60
Vegetable Casserole—Mae K. Redfield 60
Tomato Pie—Teresa Floyd 61
Squash and Cheese Casserole—Teresa Floyd 61
Squash Casserole—Decca Riedel 61
Sweet Potato Casserole—Vicki Taylor 62

Roasted Sweet Potato Wedges—
Carolyn Price 62
Roasted Vegetables—Catherine Dancy 63
Garlic Rosemary Potatoes—Carolyn Price 63
Gratin of Root Vegetables—Julie James 64
Spicy Cauliflower and Potatoes—
Andrea Morgan 64
Mushroom Rice—Judy Prater, Betsy Hensley 65
Ranch Style Baked Beans ☘—Bob May 65
Athens Greek Couscous—Julie Walker 66
Garlic Cheese Grits—Lara Luck 66
Tabouleh—Laura Weigand 67
Baked Fruit Compote—Mitzi Loflin Sapp 67
Pineapple Casserole—Rob Norwood 68
Cranberry Relish—Elizabeth Skinner 68

BREADS 69

Broccoli Corn Bread—Hazel Myers,
Gladys R. Dunnagan, Jacquelyn Smith 70
Southern Corn Bread—Mary McAfee 71
Virginia Spoon Bread—Lise Keppler 71
Advent Bread ☘—Jane Hill 72
Cool Rise Bread ☘—Bill Sugg 73
Granny Rolls—Lise Keppler 74
Ice Box Rolls—Donna L. Staley 74
Tender Dinner Knots—Juanita A. Tatum 75
Quick and Easy Herb Bread—Yolanda Pickett 75
Mom's Whole Wheat Bread—Mary McAfee 76

CAKES 77

Apple Pound Cake—Hazel Myers 78
Big Mama's Apple Cake—Merrikay Brown 78
Fresh Apple Cake—Vicki H. Davis 79
Best Coconut Cake—Elaine Childress 79
Orange Coconut Cake—Merrikay Brown 80
Seven-Minute Frosting—Merrikay Brown 81
Big Mama's Lemon Pound Cake—
Sylvia Sprinkle-Hamlin 81
Lemon Frosting—Sylvia Sprinkle-Hamlin 82
Cherry Pound Cake ☘—Jane Jester 82
Cherry Frosting ☘—Jane Jester 83
7-Up® Pound Cake—Annie Johnson 83
Chocolate on Chocolate Cake—Valena V. Vogler 84
Six-Minute Chocolate Cake—Andrea Morgan 84
Toll House® Cake—Vicki Taylor 85
Rich and Creamy Chocolate Frosting—
Vicki Taylor 85
Lane Cake—Merrikay Brown 86
Italian Cream Cake—Judy Prater 87
Cream Cheese Frosting –Judy Prater,
Elizabeth Skinner 87
Sock-It-To-Me Cake ☘—Mary Dula 88
Strawberry Shortcake ☘—Butch Allred 88
Three Sisters' Carrot Cake—Elizabeth Skinner 89
Southern Gingerbread and Lemon Sauce—
Kathleen Wheeless 90
Pumpkin Crisp Cake—Brenda Israel 91
Rum Cake—Claudette Weston 91
Cream Cheese Cake ☘—Jean Godfrey Block 92
Robert's Ginger Cheesecake—Robert Burgin 92

PIES 93

Apple Pie—Dare Reich 94
French Cherry Pie—Elizabeth Skinner 94
Frozen Lemonade Pie—Wendy Bright 95
Strawberry Pie—Judy Prater 95
Million Dollar Pie ☘—Gladys Edwards 96
Jennifer's Favorite Pumpkin Pie—
Jennifer Wiseman 96
Mrs. Williams's Pumpkin Pie—Melisa Williams 97
Grandmother Wheeless's Pumpkin Pie—
Kathleen Wheeless 98
Sweet Potato Pie—Rob Norwood 98
Satia's Sweet Potato Pie—Satia Orange 99
Coconut Pie—Rob Norwood 99
Chocolate Chess Pie—Rob Norwood 100
Pecan Pie—Barbara Rickert 100

COOKIES & BROWNIES 101

Banana Oatmeal Cookies—Ramona Litcher 102
Oatmeal Walnut Cookies—Carol Brown 102
Old Fashioned Oatmeal Cookies—Matt Shaw 103
Indian Boiled Cookies ☘—Valena V. Vogler
Sesame Cookies ☘—Gerry Eggleston 104

Peanut Butter Chocolate Chip Cookies—Rob Norwood 104
Dena Southard's Ginger Snaps—Lise Keppler 105
Marcia Bernsten's English Toffee Cookies—Lise Keppler 105
Butterscotch Brownies—Emily Williams 106
Strong Girl Brownies—Cal Shepard 106
Turtle Brownies—Jacquelyn Smith 107
Summit Lemon Squares—Emily Williams 107
Lemon Bars—Vivian Taylor 108

OTHER SWEETS 109

Easy Rice Pudding 'Comfort Food'—Mary Tucker 110
Banana Pudding—Vicki Taylor 110
Mocha Charlottes—Merrikay Brown 111
Persimmon Pudding—Merrikay Brown 111
Sweet Potato Dumplings—Vivian Taylor 112
Peach Praline Cobbler—Thomasina Hawkins 112
Toffee or Pecan Pastries—Merrikay Brown 113
French Vanilla Ice Cream—Juanita A. Tatum 113
Mother's Ice Cream Crunch—Mitzi Loflin Sapp 114
Fruit and Angel Dessert—Mitzi Loflin Sapp 114
Granny's Cherry Yum-Yum—Judy Fishel Joyce 115
Peach Delight—Donna L. Staley 115
Peach Delight with Pineapple—Judy Fishel Joyce 116
Pistachio Dessert ☘—Wanda Wadkins 116
Strawberry Cream ☘—Ann Gehlen 117
Sweet Pecans—Merrikay Brown 117
Haystacks—Lara Luck 118
Bourbon Fudge—Julie James 118

BEVERAGES 119

Cheerwine® Punch—Jackie Jones 120
Cinnamon Punch—DeLois Cue 120
Citrus Mint Tea Cooler—Janelle Kent 120
Lime Freeze Punch—Mary Dula 121
Jennifer Huffingham's Russian Tea Mix—Elizabeth Skinner 121
Al Sooman's Christmas Punch ☘—Bill Roberts 122
Close to 'South by Southwest' Cactus Nectar Margarita—Dave Fergusson 122
Peach Mimosas—Jenny Barrett 123
Colombian Sangria—Julie Walker 123
Hot Scotch—Teresa Floyd 124

BREAKFAST 125

Always Perfect Banana Bread—Elizabeth Skinner 126
Banana Bread—Mackenzie Krell 126
Banana Muffins—Barbara Hill 127
Zucchini Bread—Kathleen Wheeless 127
Easy Scones—Dr. Tom Shown 128
Orange-Scented Scones—Ben Morgan 128
Orange Scones—Susan Peterson 129
Blueberry Buckle—Julie James 129
Moravian Sugar Cake—Nancy Metzgar 130
Quick Coffee Cake—Ben Morgan 130
Breakfast Smoothie—Jessica Cole 131
Breakfast Casserole—Betsy Hensley 131
Cheddarliscious Egg and Sausage Casserole—Arneita Hairston 131
Sausage Cheese Muffins—Teresa Floyd 132
Quiche Formula—Julie James 132

ACKNOWLEDGMENTS 135

INDEX 137

FOREWORD

On February 14, 1906, the Carnegie Library opened for business on the corner of Cherry and Third Streets in the City of Winston. Since then, millions of county residents have passed through the public library doors. Tens of millions of items have circulated, millions of reference questions have been answered, tens of thousands of public programs have been presented, thousands of Forsyth County Public Library employees have come and gone, and countless recipes have been exchanged among library staff, trustees and library lovers.

This cookbook seeks to preserve some of those recipes for purposes both culinary and historic.

A Tasteful Century reaches you through the efforts of an energetic band of kitchen-savvy, food-loving librarians who saw in it a fun and practical way of contributing to Forsyth County Public Library's year-long centennial celebration.

Proceeds from the sale of this book will be used to purchase materials and enhance technology for the library. Buying this book allows one to be simultaneously kind to one's palate and generous to one's library.

There is also historical precedent for the publication of a centennial cookbook. Thirty years ago, FCPL staff celebrated the nation's bi-centennial by compiling the booklet *Favorite Recipes: Forsyth County Public Library Staff 1976*. *A Tasteful Century* includes some recipes from that 1976 publication. It also lets us hear from 1906 Library Procurement Committee Chair, Mrs. J. Lindsay Patterson, and several of her designated subject specialists whose recipes are reproduced here as they appeared in *The Twin-City Housewife, 5th edition* (a publication of The Whatsoever Circle of the North Carolina Branch of King's Daughters in Winston-Salem, circa 1914).

Contributors to *A Tasteful Century* include library staff, trustees and friends, past and present. More than anything, though, this book represents a one hundred year collaboration of people who enjoy good food and love the Forsyth County Public Library.

I hope you'll find the mix delectable.

Sylvia Sprinkle-Hamlin
Director of Libraries
September 1, 2006

Forsyth County Public Library
Celebrate a Century!

Winston-Salem, North Carolina
www.forsythlibrary.org

From the Winston-Salem Journal
Vol. VII. No. 94.
Thursday Morning, September 14 1905

FOR THE LIBRARY

COMMITTEES APPOINTED FOR PURCHASE OF BOOKS.

OPENING NEXT THURSDAY

Mrs. J. Lindsay Patterson and Her Assistants Met Yesterday Afternoon to Discuss Ways and Means to "Furnish" the Carnegie Structure and Expend the $1,200 Appropriation Most Wisely.

The meeting in the interest of the Carnegie Library, in regard to the best books to procure, and ways and means of procuring them was held yesterday afternoon at 3:30 o'clock at Mrs. W. N. Reynolds' apartments, at the Hotel Phoenix. Mrs. Lindsay Patterson, chairman of committee, presiding. The attendance was quite large attesting the great interest of our people in this cause which is truly for the uplifting and entertainment of the Winston-Salem people of all classes.

The most feasible plan of putting to the best use the $1200 appropriative was discussed, and finally decided upon. Mrs. Patterson delegating the following sub committees, each of which is to work up its subject thoroughly, make a list of the best books under its head, and present the same for discussion at the next meeting next Wednesday afternoon at 3 o'clock.

The following are the committees appointed by Mrs. Patterson:

Literature of North Carolina, including its histories, Prof. Leon Cash as chairman.
Biography, Mrs. Mitchell Rogers, chairman.
History, Mrs. A. H. Eller, chairman.
Modern Fiction, Mrs. Clement Manly, chairman.
Fine Arts, Mrs. Clay Lilly, chairman.
General Literature, Mr. H. R. Dwire, chairman.
Travel, and Poetry, Mrs. L. A. Vaughn and Mrs. A. V. Maslin.
Nature Books and Studies, Miss Eleanor Follin, chairman.
Best books for children, Prof. W. S. Snipes.

All of these committees are asked to have their lists ready by the next meeting which will be at Mrs. W. N. Reynolds' apartments at the Hotel Phoenix. On Thursday night of next week the Carnegie Library of Winston-Salem is so justly pround, will be thrown open to the public, and a general reception will be held.

It is earnestly requested of every one that he or she bring one book or several to go to upbuilding the library. This is not at all necessary for admission and a cordial welcome to the opening, but it is a suggestion urged upon sensible grounds.

Editor's note: Many of the women active in the library procurement effort were members of King's Daughters, a nondenominational, philanthropic organization founded by churchwomen in New York City in 1886. The North Carolina Branch was established in 1890 and is still in existence although there is no longer a circle in Winston-Salem.

The Whatsover Circle of the North Carolina Branch of King's Daughters in Winston-Salem published several editions of a cookbook titled The Twin-City Housewife. We're very pleased to offer some of the recipes provided by Mrs. J. Lindsay Patterson, chairman of the library procurement committee, and several of her delegated subject specialists that were included in the book.

The following recipes are found in the fifth edition, believed to date to approximately 1914. We are grateful to librarian John Via for sharing this wonderful resource from his personal collection and for finding the article reproduced above.

THE TWIN-CITY HOUSEWIFE

Edited by Whatsoever Circle, King's Daughters
Winston-Salem, N.C.

With apron neat and face so sweet,
It pays all eyes for looking,
The Southern wife, as sure as life,
Can beat the world on cooking.

Fried chicken's name she gilds with fame,
For baked beans and bread—see Boston;
Let who will sigh for arts gone by,
This art is not a lost one.

I've feasted North, I've feasted West,
I've starved on foreign menu—
North Carolina's cooks of all are best;
Come, try the ways that they knew.

—Mrs. W. L. Hill

FISH A LA CREME, NO. 2

One pint of pieces of cold cooked fish, yolks of two eggs, one pint of milk, one blade of mace, one bay leaf, a sprig of parsley, a small piece of onion, one large tablespoon of butter, seven tablespoons of flour. Put the milk in a boiler, add to it the onion, mace, parsley and bay leaf, and let it stand until boiling hot. Put the butter in a frying pan to melt without browning; add the flour; stir until thoroughly mixed. Strain into it the milk, stirring continuously until it boils. Take from the fire, add a teaspoon of salt, one-quarter teaspoon of pepper, and the well-beaten yolks. Add the fish carefully and turn the whole into a baking dish, or small individual dishes, sprinkle the top with bread crumbs and bits of butter and put in the oven a few minutes to brown. –Mrs. Lindsay Patterson.

SPICED BEEF

Boil four or five pounds of beef until the meat falls off the bone. Shred the meat and chop the soft gristle very fine. Set aside the liquor in which the meat was boiled until cold; then skim the fat off and boil down to one pint. Roll six crackers fine and add to the meat. Pour all into the hot liquor, adding salt, pepper and a pinch each of ground cloves, cinnamon and nutmeg. Let it boil up once. Put in a mould with a weight upon it. Cut in thin slices and serve. –Mrs. A. V. Maslin.

BEATEN BISCUIT, NO. 1

Put one and one-half teaspoons of salt into a quart and a half of finest flour. Sift twice and mix thoroughly with a teacup of lard. Moisten with ice water, which add slowly until a stiff dough is formed; knead until the dough blisters, then roll out to the thickness of about one-half inch, cut with a small cutter and bake in a steady, strong oven. –Mrs. L. A. Vaughan.

FRUIT CAKE

One pound of flour, one pound sugar, three-fourths of a pound of butter, ten eggs, three pounds of raisins, one pound currants, one pound citron, one pound almonds, blanched and powdered, and one pound English walnuts. Dredge all the fruit and nuts thoroughly, but use extra flour, not disturbing the pound weighed out for the batter. Two large nutmegs grated, three tablespoons cinnamon, two of cloves and one teaspoon of spice, one small teacup of brandy, a teacup of sherry and two tablespoons of extract of lemon. Make a batter as for pound cake, add the dredged fruits and nuts, with seasoning mixed in, then the lemon and brandy, and lastly the wine, with a teaspoon of soda stirred in and allowed to foam. Grease the mould thoroughly and line bottom with four or five layers of paper, likewise tie several thicknesses of same around the sides of mould. Lay a paper over the top and bake about four hours. –Mrs. L. A. Vaughn.

PINEAPPLE PUDDING, NO. 1

One pint grated pineapple, one cup of sugar, four eggs (beaten together), one cup of cream or rich milk. Stir all well together and pour into a buttered mould. Set mould in pan of warm water and bake until firm and brown. Serve with whipped cream. –Mrs. A. H. Eller.

The following recipe is handwritten on the last page of the book, presumably by the unknown owner of the volume. Might this be the origin of Winston-Salem's own Krispy Kreme® doughnuts?

DOUGHNUTS

Melt three tablespoons of butter and add one cupful of sugar, two eggs, well beaten, and one cupful of milk. Then add four cupfuls of flour, mixed and sifted with five teaspoonfuls of salt and a few grains of nutmeg. Toss on a floured board, knead slightly and pat and roll to one fourth inch in thickness, using one third the mixture at a time. Shape with a doughnut cutter, remove to floured tin sheet. When all are cut, fry in deep fat and drain on brown paper. Doughnuts should come quickly to top of fat, brown on one side then be turned to brown on the other side. Fat must be kept at a uniform temperature. If not hot, doughnuts will brown before sufficiently risen. If not hot enough they will absorb fat.

NOTES TO THIS VOLUME

ABBREVIATIONS USED

Volume

tsp.	teaspoon
Tbsp.	tablespoon
oz.	fluid ounce
c.	cup
pt.	pint
qt.	quart
ltr.	liter

Weight

oz.	ounce
lb.	pound

Size

sm.	small
med.	medium
lg.	large

STANDARD SIZES

Unless stated otherwise, the following standard sizes are assumed:

canned legumes	14-16 oz. (1¾ c.)
canned soups	10.5-12 oz. (1¼ c.)
canned vegetables	14-16 oz. (1¾ c.)
dry mixes, cake	18-18.5 oz.
dry mixes, corn muffin	8.5 oz.
dry mixes, flavored gelatin, regular	3 oz.
dry mixes, flavored gelatin, sugar-free	.25-.35 oz.
dry mixes, instant pudding	3.4 oz.
dry mixes, onion soup	1 oz.
eggs	large (24 oz. per dozen)
frozen vegetables	10 oz.
pie crust, frozen deep dish	8 oz.
pie crust, frozen standard	7.5 oz.
pie crust, graham cracker	6 oz.
pie crust, refrigerated	8 oz.

"Half the cookbooks tell you how to cook the food and the other half tell you how to avoid eating it."
Andy Rooney, 1919–

NUTRITION

Nutrition facts are calculated using U.S.D.A. values for ingredients. Actual values may vary depending on ingredients used, preparation methods and serving sizes.

Calories

To lower the calories in a recipe, consider reducing fats and sugars (see below) or serving smaller portions. Many of the prepared products used in these recipes are available in reduced calorie versions. Lower calorie substitutes may be used successfully in most cases although flavors and textures may be altered.

Fats

Along with butter, margarine, shortening and oils, cheeses and nuts significantly increase the fat content in foods. To lower the fat, consider using reduced fat or fat-free substitutes or cutting back on the quantity of high-fat ingredients.

Sugars

Although the chemistry of candies and most baked goods requires some form of sugar, non-nutritive sweeteners such as saccharin, aspartame and sucralose may be used in many recipes. Any recipe that calls for flavored gelatin, for example, may be made with a sugar-free variety.

Sodium

Many prepared foods included in these recipes contain high levels of sodium. To lower the sodium content, consider using reduced salt or salt-free varieties of canned foods. Be aware that this will affect the flavor. Salt substitutes, such as Mrs. Dash® and Nu-Salt®, may be used in many recipes or herbs and spices may be added to boost flavor. Do not make substitutions in baked goods as salt may be necessary for proper chemical action.

APPETIZERS

Baked Onion Dip

1 c. mayonnaise
1 c. chopped onion
¼ tsp. garlic salt
1 c. shredded Swiss cheese

Preheat oven to 325ºF. Mix all ingredients together. Spoon into 1-quart baking dish. Bake uncovered for 40 minutes. Serve with crackers.

Nutrition facts per serving: 92 calories; 2.6 g protein; 7.2 g fat; 4.7 g carbohydrates; 0.2 g fiber; 140 mg sodium. 16 servings.

Teresa Floyd, current staff

Black Bean Hummus

1 clove garlic
1 Tbsp. olive oil
1 can black beans, rinsed and drained
1 tsp. paprika
1 to 2 Tbsp. lemon juice
dash cayenne pepper
½ tsp. sea salt
¼ to ⅓ c. water

Process all ingredients in food processor and chill.

Nutrition facts per serving: 116 calories; 6.6 g protein; 2.2 g fat; 18.5 g carbohydrates; 6.7 g fiber; 324 mg sodium. 8 servings.

Ben Morgan, current staff

Bonnie's Clam Dip

6.5-oz. can clams
8 oz. cream cheese, softened
1½ Tbsp. fine herbs (French herb blend; if not available, use Herbes de Provence blend)
½ to ¾ Tbsp. garlic pepper
½ c. mayonnaise

Drain clams and reserve juice. In small saucepan, heat cream cheese with 2 Tbsp. clam juice. Stir until smooth. Add clams, spices and mayonnaise and mix. Chill overnight.

Nutrition facts per serving: 113 calories; 2.6 g protein; 9.9 g fat; 4.0 g carbohydrates; 0.4 g fiber; 274 mg sodium. 12 servings.

Bonnie Fulp, former staff member in Business & Science, was often asked to bring this.
Kathleen Wheeless, current staff

Spinach Artichoke Dip

3 boxes frozen chopped spinach, thawed
1 c. reduced-fat sour cream
½ c. grated Parmesan cheese
8 oz. cream cheese, softened
1 c. shredded mozzarella cheese, divided
4 cloves fresh garlic, crushed
½ tsp. ground pepper
2 tsp. hot pepper sauce (or more to taste)
1 can artichoke hearts, drained

Preheat oven to 350ºF. Squeeze all excess liquid from spinach. Place spinach in food processor with sour cream, Parmesan, cream cheese, ½ cup of mozzarella, garlic, pepper and hot sauce. Process until well blended but still slightly lumpy. Add artichokes and pulse to form chunky mixture. Place in 1-quart baking dish. Top with remaining mozzarella. Bake until bubbly, about 30 minutes. Serve with carrot sticks, celery sticks or baked tortilla chips.

Nutrition facts per serving: 123 calories; 6.0 g protein; 9.6 g fat; 4.9 g carbohydrates; 2.7 g fiber; 243 mg sodium. 16 servings.

This recipe is from John, the chef at 6th and Vine
Kathleen Wheeless, current staff

"Artichokes are just plain annoying. After all the trouble you go to, you get about as much actual 'food' out of eating an artichoke as you would from licking thirty or forty postage stamps. Have the shrimp cocktail instead."

Miss Piggy, timeless

Julie's Guacamole

1 sweet onion, quartered
1 bunch fresh cilantro
½ tsp. salt
1 fresh jalapeño pepper, seeded (handle with gloves!)
2 roma tomatoes
1 ripe avocado

Place onion, cilantro, salt and jalapeño in small food processor and chop until fine. Dice tomatoes and avocado, place in bowl and add cilantro mixture. Stir, slightly mashing avocado, until you have chunky texture. Serve immediately. Never refrigerate!

Nutrition facts per serving: 109 calories; 2.4 g protein; 7.6 g fat; 10.1 g carbohydrates; 3.9 g fiber; 308 mg sodium. 4 servings.

Julie Walker, former staff and current PINES Program Director, Georgia Public Library Service

Dip for Tortilla Chips

- 8 oz. cream cheese, softened
- 15-oz. can Hormel® chili with beans
- 2 sm. onions, chopped
- 8 oz. cheddar cheese, shredded

Preheat oven to 350ºF. Spread cream cheese in bottom of 9″x9″ pan. Layer remaining ingredients in order given. Bake for 20 minutes.

Nutrition facts per serving: 187 calories; 9.0 g protein; 13.3 g fat; 7.5 g carbohydrates; 1.6 g fiber; 368 mg sodium. 12 servings.

Judy Prater, current staff

Easy Mexican Dip

- 8 oz. cream cheese, softened
- 16-oz. can refried beans
- 2 small (3.25-oz.) cans chopped black olives
- 1 small (7-oz.) can chopped green chili peppers
- 16-oz. jar salsa
- 2 c. grated cheese

Preheat oven to 350ºF. Layer all ingredients in 9″x13″ dish in order given. Bake for 30 minutes. Delicious served with tortilla chips.

Nutrition facts per serving: 210 calories; 8.3 g protein; 14.2 g fat; 11.2 g carbohydrates; 2.7 g fiber; 654 mg sodium. 12 servings.

We serve this a lot during any holiday because it is so quick and easy. It came from my sister.
Judy Fishel Joyce, member Forsyth County Public Library Board of Trustees

Layered Taco Dip

- 8 oz. cream cheese, softened
- 8 oz. sour cream
- 1 pkg. taco seasoning mix
- 8 oz. chunky salsa
- 1 or 2 tomatoes, diced
- 1 head lettuce, shredded
- 8 oz. grated cheddar cheese

Combine cream cheese, sour cream and taco seasoning and mix until well blended. Spread onto bottom of 9″ pie plate. Layer remaining ingredients, ending with lettuce and cheese on top. You may add other ingredients such as green pepper, black olives, bacon bits, diced jalapeños, etc. Serve with tortilla chips. Enjoy!

Nutrition facts per serving: 155 calories; 5.1 g protein; 12.6 g fat; 4.8 g carbohydrates; 0.6 g fiber; 386 mg sodium. 16 servings.

Jennifer Wiseman, Friend of the Lewisville Library

Margot Wharton's Tex-Mex Dip

3 ripe avocados
2 Tbsp. lemon juice
½ tsp. salt
¼ tsp. ground pepper
1 c. sour cream
½ c. mayonnaise
1 pkg. taco seasoning mix
21-oz. can bean dip with jalapeño peppers
1 bunch scallions, diced
2 fresh tomatoes, cubed
7 oz. pitted ripe olives, sliced
8 oz. sharp cheddar cheese, shredded

Mash avocados with lemon juice, salt and pepper. In separate bowl, combine sour cream, mayonnaise and taco seasoning. Layer casserole in this order: bean dip, avocado mixture, sour cream mixture, scallions, tomatoes, olives and cheese. Chill overnight. Serve with tortilla chips.

Nutrition facts per serving: 238 calories; 6.4 g protein; 16.4 g fat; 16.7 g carbohydrates; 5.0 g fiber; 802 mg sodium. 16 servings.

Margot Wharton worked in First Line during the 1980s.
Kathleen Wheeless, current staff

Joy White's Spinach Spread

1 box frozen chopped spinach
⅔ c. mayonnaise or plain yogurt
½ tsp. salt
½ tsp. ground pepper
1 c. chopped fresh parsley
⅓ to ½ c. chopped spring onions

Thaw spinach and squeeze out excess moisture. Combine all ingredients. Cover and store overnight in refrigerator to allow flavors to blend. Serve with crackers, baguette slices or raw veggies.

Nutrition facts per serving (made with mayonnaise): 60 calories; 1.0 g protein; 4.4 g fat; 4.4 g carbohydrates; 0.9 g fiber; 211 mg sodium.
Per serving (made with yogurt): 20 calories; 1.5 g protein; 0.7 g fat; 2.2 g carbohydrates; 0.9 g fiber; 127 mg sodium.
12 servings.

Joy White worked at FCPL in the 1970s and 80s. She often brought this spread to library parties.
Karen Robertson, current staff

"Don't let love interfere with your appetite. It never does with mine."

Anthony Trollope, 1815-1882

Blue Cheese Ball

8 oz. cream cheese, softened
8 oz. blue cheese, crumbled
½ stick (4 Tbsp.) butter, softened
2 Tbsp. dry sherry
½ c. chopped pecans or walnuts

Mix cheeses, butter and sherry. Chill until firm enough to handle. Form into 2 balls and roll in nuts.

Nutrition facts per serving: 151 calories; 4.4 g protein; 14.3 g fat; 1.7 g carbohydrates; 0.3 g fiber; 268 mg sodium. 16 servings.

Marty Reith, former staff

Spicy Cheese Log

8 oz. cream cheese, softened
1 tsp. Worcestershire sauce
¼ tsp. cayenne pepper
10 oz. extra-sharp cheddar cheese, shredded
8 oz. Monterey jack cheese with peppers, shredded
1 c. toasted pecans or walnuts, chopped
½ c. chopped fresh parsley
fresh parsley sprigs for garnish

Combine first3ingredients in large bowl and blend well. Stir in shredded cheeses. Divide cheese mixture in half and shape each portion into 8″ log. Combine nuts and chopped parsley. Roll logs in nut mixture. Cover and chill for 8 hours. Let stand 1 hour before serving. Garnish with parsley sprigs and serve with crackers.

Nutrition facts per serving: 149 calories; 6.4 g protein; 13.3 g fat; 1.1 g carbohydrates; 0.5 g fiber; 164 mg sodium. 24 servings.

Adapted from recipe found in Christmas with Southern Living: 2004
Carole Bonnell, current staff

Pepperoni Cheese Ball

16 oz. cream cheese, softened
8 oz. pepperoni, chopped
8-oz. can crushed juice-pack pineapple, drained
¾ tsp. seasoned salt
⅓ c. finely chopped green pepper
1 tsp. onion salt

Mix all ingredients in large bowl. Shape into 1 large or 2 small balls. Chill until firm. Note: May be rolled in portion of chopped pepperoni.

Nutrition facts per serving: 116 calories; 3.0 g protein; 10.7 g fat; 2.5 g carbohydrates; 0 g fiber; 335 mg sodium. 24 servings.

Jennifer Wiseman, Friend of the Lewisville Library. "I think the staff is just the greatest! I am proud to call them my friends."

Salmon Ball

1 lg. (14.75-oz.) can pink salmon, drained
8 oz. light cream cheese, softened
1 Tbsp. lemon juice
2 tsp. grated onion
¼ tsp. salt
¼ tsp. liquid smoke
1 c. chopped nuts
¼ c. parsley flakes

Combine all ingredients except chopped nuts and parsley. Mix thoroughly. Refrigerate about 8 hours. Shape into ball and roll in mixture of chopped nuts and parsley. Note: Measure liquid smoke over sink, not over bowl. It's very strong and you don't want to spill any into salmon mixture.

Nutrition facts per serving: 179 calories; 11.0 g protein; 14.4 g fat; 2.4 g carbohydrates; 1.0 g fiber; 246 mg sodium. 12 servings.

Barbara Anderson, current staff

"i have noticed
that when
chickens quit
quarrelling over their
food they often
find that there is
enough for all of them
i wonder if
it might not
be the same way
with the human race"

Don Marquis, 1878-1937
archys life of mehitabel

Cheese Krispies

2 sticks (1 c.) margarine, melted
2 c. all-purpose flour
2 c. shredded sharp cheese
½ tsp. salt
½ tsp. crushed or flaked red pepper
2 c. Rice Krispies® cereal

Preheat oven to 350°F. Mix all ingredients together, adding Rice Krispies® last. Form into 1" balls. Place on greased cookie sheet and mash with fork to flatten. Bake for 10 to 12 minutes until lightly brown. Note: Can be frozen and baked when thawed. (Editor's note: Amount of cheese can be increased if you like more intense flavor.)

Nutrition facts per item: 76 calories; 1.8 g protein; 5.4 g fat; 5.0 g carbohydrates; 0.1 g fiber; 104 mg sodium. 4 dozen.

Sharon Watts, current staff

Cheese Pennies

1 stick (½ c.) butter, softened
4 oz. grated cheddar cheese
½ pkg. dry onion soup mix
½ tsp. salt
1 c. all-purpose flour

Cream butter with cheese. Add onion soup mix, salt and flour. Blend well. Shape into 1″ roll. Wrap in waxed paper and refrigerate until well chilled. Preheat oven to 375ºF. Cut roll in ¼″ slices and bake on ungreased cookie sheet for about 10 minutes or until lightly browned. Check pennies as they bake since overcooking can develop a somewhat bitter taste. Notes: Have cheese well chilled before grating—it makes the job easier. But have butter and cheese at room temperature before creaming.

Nutrition facts per piece: 38 calories; 1.0 g protein; 2.7 g fat; 2.4 g carbohydrates; 0.1 g fiber; 131 mg sodium. 4 dozen pieces.

Anne Correll, former staff

"Now good digestion wait on appetite,
And good health on both!"

William Shakespeare, 1564-1616
Macbeth, Act III, Scene iv

Crabbies

6 English muffins, sliced
6.5-oz. can crabmeat, drained and cleaned
5 oz. jar Kraft Old English® cheese spread
1 stick (½ c.) butter, softened
¼ tsp. garlic powder

Preheat oven to 400ºF. Lightly toast English muffins. Mix all remaining ingredients together until smooth and creamy. Divide mixture evenly over muffins and spread to edges. Cut each muffin into 4 equal triangles and place on cookie sheet. Bake for 15 minutes and serve hot. Crabbies can be frozen before baking.

Nutrition facts per serving: 183 calories; 7.2 g protein; 10.7 g fat; 13.9 g carbohydrates; 0.8 g fiber; 416 mg sodium. 12 servings.

This recipe came from a computer programmer in Boston. She was quiet and shy but threw a terrific party!
Lise Keppler, current staff

Spinach Tortilla Roll-Ups

2 pkgs. frozen chopped spinach, thawed
6 green onions, chopped
8 oz. light mayonnaise
8 oz. reduced-fat sour cream
3-oz. jar Hormel® bacon bits
1 sm. pkg. Hidden Valley® buttermilk ranch dressing mix
1 lg. pkg. (8 to10) medium flour tortillas

Squeeze excess water from spinach and pull apart in shreds. Mix with remaining ingredients except tortillas. Spread mixture on tortillas and roll up. Refrigerate at least 6 hours or overnight. Slice into bite-size pieces to serve.

Nutrition facts per serving: 118 calories; 4.0 g protein; 6.5 g fat; 11.0 g carbohydrates; 1.9 g fiber; 396 mg sodium. 24 servings.

This recipe came from my mother-in-law in California.
Sandy Dwyer, Friend of the Library and Co-Director of West Central area for FONCPL

Asparagus Rolls

½ stick (4 Tbsp.) butter
2 Tbsp. all-purpose flour
1 c. milk
½ tsp. salt
1 c. grated cheddar cheese
16 spears cooked or canned asparagus
4 thin slices boiled ham
4 slices bread

Preheat oven to 400°F. Melt butter in heavy saucepan. Add flour, milk and salt, stirring constantly, to make basic white sauce. Add cheese and heat to melt. Wrap 4 spears asparagus in each ham slice and place in baking dish. Cover with cheese sauce. Bake for 15 minutes. Toast bread and cut into triangles. Arrange toast pieces on 4 hors d'oeuvres plates. Place asparagus bundles on top of toast and serve.

Nutrition facts per serving: 407 calories; 22.9 g protein; 26.3 g fat; 22.5 g carbohydrates; 2.6 g fiber; 1604 mg sodium. 4 servings.

Diane Burrows, former staff

Sweet and Sour Avocados

4 strips bacon
4 Tbsp. butter or margarine
2 Tbsp. granulated sugar
2 Tbsp. catsup
2 Tbsp. red wine vinegar
½ Tbsp. soy sauce
2 avocados
lemon juice (approx. 1 Tbsp.)

Chop bacon and sauté until crisp. Remove from pan and drain on paper towels. Melt butter in small saucepan. Add sugar, catsup, vinegar and soy sauce, stirring over low heat until sugar is dissolved. Keep warm or reheat later over low heat. Just before serving, cut avocadoes in half, remove pits and sprinkle with lemon juice. Put bacon bits in cavities and pour warm sauce over top. Serve with spoon to scoop avocado out of rind and damp napkins for sticky fingers.

Nutrition facts per serving: 289 calories; 2.4 g protein; 27.0 g fat; 14.7 g carbohydrates; 4.1 g fiber; 342 mg sodium. 4 servings.

Dolores Sampedro, current staff

Bob Rickert's Shrimp Cocktail Sauce

12-oz. bottle Heinz® chili sauce
2 Tbsp. water to rinse out bottle
2½ tsp. fresh lemon juice
1 tsp. Worcestershire sauce
1 or 2 packets Equal® artificial sweetener
1 tsp. garlic powder
½ tsp. celery salt

Blend all ingredients. Refrigerate. Makes enough for 2 lbs. chilled cooked shrimp.

Nutrition facts per serving: 31 calories; 0.7 g protein; 0.1 g fat; 6.1 g carbohydrates; 1.7 g fiber; 482 mg sodium. 12 servings.

Original recipe. Good sharp flavor and no horseradish!
Barbara and Bob Rickert, Friends of the Library. "Everyone is so helpful."

SALADS

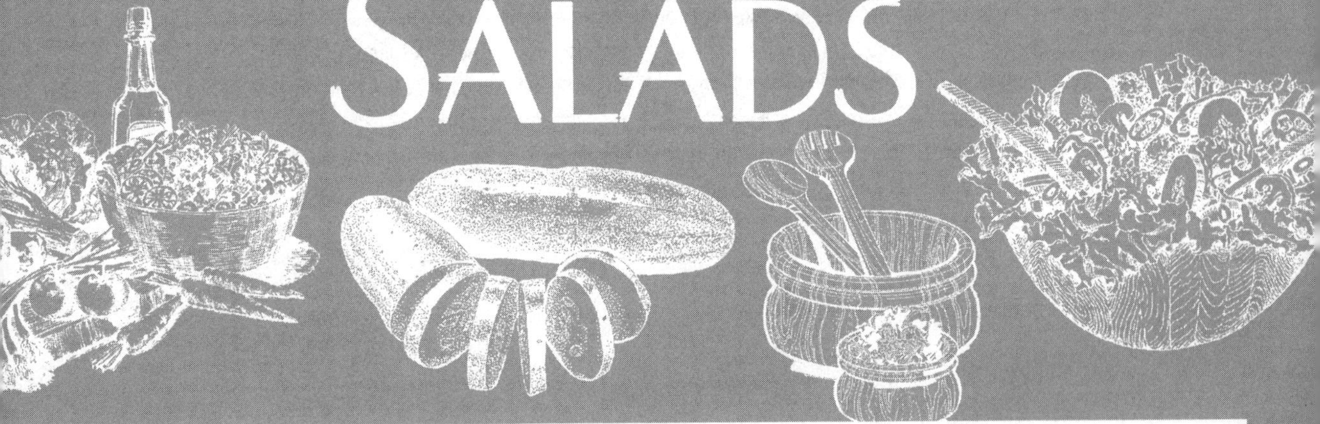

Broad Bean Salad (Fool Midammis)

1 c. dried small fava or broad beans
1 Tbsp. dried red lentils
1 qt. water
¼ c. olive oil
1 Tbsp. fresh lemon juice
½ tsp. salt
1 Tbsp. finely chopped fresh parsley (preferably flat-leaf variety)
8 pitted black olives

Wash beans and lentils in colander set under cold running water until water runs clear. Drain thoroughly. In large heavy pot, bring water to boil over high heat. Add beans and lentils, reduce heat to low and partially cover pot. Simmer for 3 to 4 hours or until beans are tender and show no resistance when pressed gently between your fingers. Check from time to time to make sure that beans are moist. Add a few tablespoons of boiling water if necessary. When beans are done, there should be almost no liquid left in pot. Transfer entire contents of pot to bowl and cool to room temperature. With whisk or fork, beat oil, lemon juice and salt together. Add to beans, mashing them gently with fork and stirring until they absorb most of dressing. To serve, spread beans on platter or individual plates, sprinkle with parsley and garnish with olives.

Nutrition facts per serving: 159 calories; 2.3 g protein; 14.5 g fat; 5.7 g carbohydrates; 2.4 g fiber; 377 mg sodium. 4 servings.

Aleya El Maghrabi, former staff

Calico Salad

1 can green beans
1 can wax or yellow beans
1 can red kidney beans
1 can lima beans
1 lg. onion, thinly sliced
½ c. chopped green pepper
2 Tbsp. chopped pimento
¾ c. granulated sugar
⅓ c. vegetable oil
⅔ c. vinegar
1 tsp. salt
1 tsp. ground black pepper
¼ tsp. garlic powder (optional)

Drain all beans and combine with onion, green pepper and pimento. In separate bowl or jar, combine all remaining ingredients and stir or shake to blend. Pour dressing over vegetables and marinate for at least 24 hours. (Editor's note: Our taste tester successfully used ½ c. Splenda® artificial sweetener and ¼ c. sugar. This reduces calories to 149 per serving and carbohydrates to 19.8 g.)

Nutrition facts per serving: 181 calories; 4.4 g protein; 6.4 g fat; 28.1 g carbohydrates; 5.3 g fiber; 586 mg sodium. 12 servings.

Louise Pulley, former staff

Marinated Cucumber Salad

1 large cucumber, thinly sliced
1 small onion, thinly sliced
1 c. white vinegar
1 c. water
3/4 c. granulated sugar
1 tsp. salt
ground black pepper (optional)
1 Tbsp. dried dill, or to taste

Toss cucumber and onion together in large bowl. Combine vinegar, water, sugar, salt and pepper (if desired) in saucepan over medium-high heat. Bring to boil and pour over cucumber and onions. Stir in dill, cover and refrigerate until cold. This can also be eaten at room temperature, but be sure to allow the cucumbers to marinate for at least 1 hour, preferably overnight. Notes: If the cucumbers are too waxy, peel them in stripes, slice the whole cucumber in half, then into slices. For more flavor, substitute another type of vinegar (like cider, white wine, or rice), but then you may need to increase the water to balance it out.

Nutrition facts per serving: 56 calories; 0.6 g protein; 1.0 g fat; 14.2 g carbohydrates; 0.7 g fiber; 147 mg sodium. 4 servings.

Julie James, former staff

"My salad days,
When I was green in judgment."

William Shakespeare, 1564-1616
Antony and Cleopatra, Act I, Scene v

Marinated Cabbage Slaw

1 head cabbage, finely shredded
1 med. onion, quartered and thinly sliced
2 Tbsp. granulated sugar
¼ c. frozen apple juice concentrate, undiluted
1/3 c. cider vinegar
½ tsp. dry mustard
½ tsp. celery seed
½ tsp. salt

In large bowl, alternate layers of shredded cabbage and onion. Sprinkle sugar over top. In microwave-proof container, combine all remaining ingredients. Microwave on high until mixture boils. Immediately pour hot liquid over cabbage mixture. Cover and refrigerate. Note: This salad is best after 2 or 3 days and keeps for at least 2 weeks.

Nutrition facts per serving: 41 calories; 1.2 g protein; 0.2 g fat; 9.6 g carbohydrates; 1.9 g fiber; 112 mg sodium. 12 servings.

Adapted from a recipe published in the Winston-Salem Journal *in 1990.*
Karen Robertson, current staff

Marinated Tomatoes

4 tomatoes
¼ c. olive oil
1 Tbsp. minced fresh basil
2 Tbsp. red wine vinegar
1/8 tsp. salt (optional)
3 drops hot pepper sauce
2 cloves garlic, minced

Slice tomatoes into bowl. Combine remaining ingredients and mix well. Pour over tomatoes and chill at least 30 minutes before serving.

Nutrition facts per serving: 78 calories; 0.8 g protein; 7.0 g fat; 4.1 g carbohydrates; 1.3 g fiber; 41 mg sodium. 8 servings.

Served at Cooking With Herbs program, part of "Successful Gardening at the Library" series
Yolanda Pickett, Extension Agent, NC Cooperative Extension Service

Copper Pennies

2 lbs. carrots
2 sm. onions, sliced in rings
1 green bell pepper, sliced in rings
1 recipe French Dressing (see below)

Peel and slice carrots. Boil in lightly salted water until tender but still firm. Drain. Add onion and green pepper to carrots. Toss freshly made dressing with vegetables. Chill in refrigerator at least 12 hours, stirring occasionally. Serve at room temperature.

Nutrition facts per serving (dressed): 135 calories; 1.3 g protein; 13.0 g fat; 5.0 g carbohydrates; 2.5 g fiber; 261 mg sodium. 8 servings.

Jessica and Gail Cole, current staff and mother/volunteer

French Dressing

1 can condensed tomato soup
1 tsp. salt
½ tsp. ground pepper
1 Tbsp. Worcestershire sauce
¼ c. vegetable oil
¾ c. vinegar

Combine all ingredients in bowl or jar, mix thoroughly and chill.

Nutrition facts per serving: 45 calories; 0.3 g protein; 3.7 g fat; 3.1 g carbohydrates; 0.1 g fiber; 261 mg sodium. 16 servings.

Jessica and Gail Cole, current staff and mother/volunteer

Tossed Salad with Fruit and Nuts

10- to 12-oz. bag salad greens
1 c. sliced fresh strawberries
1/3 c. toasted pecans, coarsely chopped
1 recipe Basic Vinaigrette (see below)
other veggies as desired (optional)

Toss salad ingredients together. Right before serving, pour vinaigrette over salad and toss. Notes: I like to use romaine. Try experimenting with different fruit and nut combinations such as: apples, dried cranberries and toasted walnuts; strawberries and pine nuts; mandarin oranges and almonds.

Nutrition facts per serving (dressed): 180 calories; 1.6 g protein; 16.7 g fat; 8.1 g carbohydrates; 2.6 g fiber; 166 mg sodium. 8 servings.

Carolyn Price, current staff

Basic Vinaigrette

¼ c. olive oil
2 Tbsp. granulated sugar
2 Tbsp. tarragon vinegar
1 tsp. Tabasco® sauce
½ tsp. salt

Combine dressing ingredients and whisk or shake in a small jar. Notes: I like to use a bit less olive oil. Try other types of flavored vinegars as well.

Nutrition facts per serving: 72 calories; 0 g protein; 6.8 g fat; 3.1 g carbohydrates; 0 g fiber; 161 mg sodium. 8 servings.

Carolyn Price, current staff

Very Berry Spinach Salad

9-oz. bag fresh spinach, cleaned
2 c. fresh strawberries, sliced
3 kiwis, peeled and sliced
½ c. chopped macadamia nuts or sliced almonds (optional)
1 recipe Raspberry Vinaigrette (see next page)

Arrange spinach, fruits and nuts in salad bowl. Toss with chilled dressing just before serving.

Nutrition facts per serving (dressed): 180 calories; 1.6 g protein; 16.7 g fat; 8.1 g carbohydrates; 2.6 g fiber; 166 mg sodium. 8 servings.

Jessica Cole, current staff

Raspberry Vinaigrette

¼ c. vegetable oil
2 Tbsp. red wine vinegar
2 Tbsp. raspberry preserves

Mix dressing ingredients and refrigerate for at least 15 minutes before tossing with salad.

Nutrition facts per serving: 75 calories; 0 g protein; 6.8 g fat; 3.6 g carbohydrates; 0 g fiber; 2 mg sodium. 8 servings.

Jessica Cole, current staff

"It's difficult to think anything but pleasant thoughts while eating a homegrown tomato."

Lewis Grizzard, 1946-1994

Seven-Layer Salad

1 head lettuce, torn
8-oz. can sliced water chestnuts, drained
1 pkg. frozen peas, thawed and drained
1 c. chopped celery
1 c. chopped onion
1½ c. mayonnaise
2 Tbsp. granulated sugar
2 c. shredded cheddar cheese
1 c. real bacon bits

Layer lettuce, water chestnuts, peas, celery and onion in large glass bowl or trifle dish. Spread mayonnaise over top, sealing to edge. Sprinkle with sugar, cheese and bacon. Chill, covered for 24 hours. Note: I use red onion for color.

Nutrition facts per serving: 336 calories; 11.6 g protein; 24.3 g fat; 18.7 g carbohydrates; 2.9 g fiber; 685 mg sodium. 10 servings.

From my mother, Rosalie Luck
Lara Luck, current staff

24-Hour Salad

½ head lettuce
½ c. finely chopped onion
½ c. chopped green pepper
1 pkg. frozen peas, thawed
½ c. mayonnaise
1 Tbsp. granulated sugar
½ c. shredded cheddar cheese
½ c. crumbled bacon

Shred lettuce in bottom of dish. Add layer of onion, layer of green pepper and layer of peas. Spread layer of mayonnaise on top and sprinkle with sugar. Top with layer of grated cheddar and crumbled bacon. Let stand in refrigerator overnight.

Nutrition facts per serving: 238 calories; 12.1 g protein; 13.6 g fat; 16.7 g carbohydrates; 5.0 g fiber; 485 mg sodium. 4 servings.

Jessica Cole and Gail Cole, current staff and mother/volunteer

Low-Fat Potato Salad

1 lb. small red potatoes
salt to taste
1 med. carrot, quartered lengthwise and thinly sliced
2 stalks celery, diced
½ med. red onion
¼ c. buttermilk
1 c. reduced-fat sour cream
1 to 2 Tbsp. whole-grain Dijon-style prepared mustard
1 tsp. dried dill
2 hard-boiled eggs, quartered
black olives to garnish
paprika

Place potatoes in saucepan and cover with cold water. Bring water to simmer over medium heat, season with salt and cook until potatoes are just tender and easily pierced with fork. Remove potatoes from saucepan and rinse briefly under cool water. Add carrots to pot of water and cook until just tender, about 2 minutes. Rinse under cold water to stop cooking. Slice potatoes into ¼" rounds and place in large bowl along with carrots. Add celery and red onion and stir to combine.

Combine buttermilk, sour cream, mustard and dill in small bowl. Pour over potato mixture and toss until potatoes and vegetables are coated. Refrigerate for at least 2 hours. Garnish with eggs, black olives and paprika. Serve chilled or bring to room temperature before serving.

Nutrition facts per serving: 158 calories; 5.2 g protein; 7.0 g fat; 17.8 g carbohydrates; 2.9 g fiber; 654 mg sodium. 6 servings.

DeLois Cue, current staff

Red-Skin Potato Salad

5 large red-skin potatoes
5 hardboiled eggs, peeled and diced
¼ c. diced onion
4-oz. jar diced pimento, drained and chopped
1½ c. mayonnaise
1½ c. milk
salt and pepper to taste

Boil potatoes until done, then peel and dice. Add eggs, onion and pimento. Blend mayonnaise and milk until creamy. Pour over potato mixture and toss to mix. Add salt and pepper to taste. Note: Best if refrigerated overnight.

Nutrition facts per serving: 233 calories; 5.5 g protein; 12.9 g fat; 24.6 g carbohydrates; 1.9 g fiber; 644 mg sodium. 12 servings.

100-year-old Northern recipe that belonged to my Grandma Wimmer, and the only dish I ever made that my husband said was better than his mom's.
Sharon Watts, current staff

South of the Border Potato Salad

4 medium potatoes
⅓ c. vegetable oil
¼ c. vinegar
1 Tbsp. granulated sugar
1½ tsp. chili powder
1 tsp. seasoned salt
dash hot pepper sauce
1 sm. onion, thinly sliced and separated into rings
1 can whole kernel corn
½ c. shredded carrot
2½ c. diced green pepper
½ c. sliced pitted ripe olives

Cook potatoes in boiling salted water until tender (approximately 35 to 40 minutes). Drain, pare and cube potatoes. Combine oil, vinegar, sugar, chili powder, seasoned salt and hot pepper sauce. Pour dressing over warm potatoes, toss gently, cover and chill 1 hour. Fold in remaining ingredients and serve chilled. Garnish with additional halved ripe olives, if desired.

Nutrition facts per serving: 221 calories; 3.9 g protein; 8.4 g fat; 34.4 g carbohydrates; 5.2 g fiber; 343 mg sodium. 10 servings.

A Sunday School classmate who lived in the Southwest brought this to a potluck. It was a popular dish and she graciously shared the recipe.
Donna L. Staley, Chairman of the Forsyth County Library Board of Trustees. "The library is a safe haven for learning, using technology and smiling librarians who are always willing to serve patrons."

Orzo and Corn Off the Cob Salad

4 ears fresh corn
1¼ c. orzo, uncooked
1 c. Greek black olives, pitted and halved
1 medium red bell pepper, chopped
¼ c. thinly sliced green onions
¼ c. thinly sliced fresh basil
¼ c. finely chopped fresh parsley
¼ c. olive oil
2 Tbsp. white wine vinegar
¼ tsp. salt
¼ tsp. freshly ground black pepper

Cut corn kernels off cob and set aside. Bring large pot of lightly salted water to boil. Add orzo and cook, stirring occasionally, for about 8 or 9 minutes until just tender, adding corn for last 3 minutes. Drain well. Add olives, pepper and green onions; toss well. Add basil, parsley, oil, vinegar, salt and pepper. Toss to combine. Serve at room temperature.

Nutrition facts per serving: 173 calories; 2.4 g protein; 8.8 g fat; 21.9 g carbohydrates; 3.6 g fiber; 307 mg sodium. 8 servings.

Adapted from Better Homes and Gardens*:* August 2003
Betty Allegrone, current staff

"Rose among roots, the maiden-fair,
Wine-scented and poetic soul
Of the capacious salad bowl."

Robert Louis Stevenson, 1850-1894
Underwoods, Bk. 1

Jell-O® Salad

1 pkg. orange flavor Jell-O® gelatin
8 oz. Cool Whip® whipped topping, thawed
12 oz. cottage cheese
8-oz. can crushed juice-pack pineapple, drained
8-oz. can juice-pack mandarin oranges, drained

Mix dry Jell-O® with Cool Whip® until well blended. Add cottage cheese and drained fruit. Mix well and refrigerate overnight.

Nutrition facts per serving: 272 calories; 8.6 g protein; 8.8 g fat; 35.7 g carbohydrates; 0.2 g fiber; 272 mg sodium. 6 servings.

Sharon Watts, current staff

Joyce's Cranberry Salad

1 pkg. Jell-O® orange gelatin
1 pkg. Jell-O® raspberry gelatin
3 c. boiling water
16-oz. can whole berry cranberry sauce
8-oz. can crushed juice-pack pineapple, drained
1 c. chopped pecans

Dissolve Jell-O® in boiling water. Stir in cranberry sauce until dissolved. Add other ingredients and mix well. Chill for several hours.

Nutrition facts per serving: 288 calories; 3.3 g protein; 9.8 g fat; 48.9 g carbohydrates; 2.1 g fiber; 71 mg sodium. 8 servings.

Jennifer Wiseman, Friend of the Lewisville Library

Ambrosia

1½ c. shredded coconut
¼ c. confectioner's sugar
2 lg. Valencia oranges, peeled and sliced
3 ripe bananas, peeled and cut into thin slices
pineapple chunks, cherries, or other fruit (optional)

Combine coconut and sugar. Arrange alternate layers of each fruit in bowl. Sprinkle each layer with coconut mixture, reserving some for top. Chill well before serving.

Nutrition facts per serving (without optional fruit): 211 calories; 1.6 g protein; 8.8 g fat; 35.0 g carbohydrates; 3.5 g fiber; 62 mg sodium. 6 servings.

Adapted from The Joy of Cooking *by Irma Rombauer. Served at On The Same Page program featuring* To Kill a Mockingbird *by Harper Lee.*
Merrikay Brown, current staff

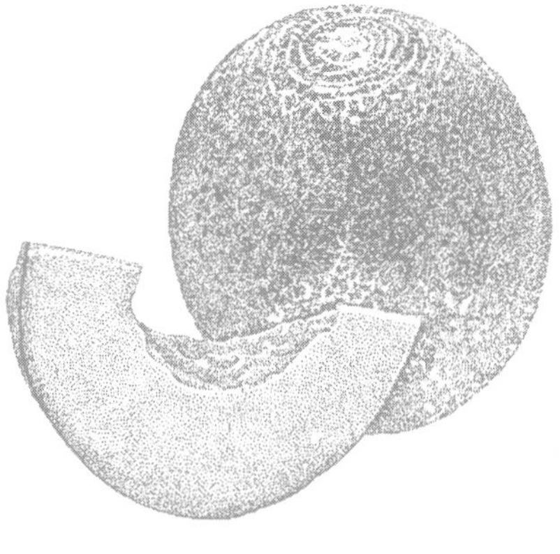

Mother Blount's Fantastic Ambrosia

8 oz. cream cheese, softened
½ c. granulated sugar
1 to 2 tsp. vanilla extract
1 c. nuts, chopped
2 sm. (11-oz.) cans juice-pack mandarin oranges, drained
10-oz. jar maraschino cherries, drained
8-oz. can crushed juice-pack pineapple or pineapple tidbits, drained
1 c. coconut
12 oz. Cool Whip® whipped topping, thawed

Mix softened cream cheese, sugar and vanilla with mixer in large bowl. Stir in all other ingredients except Cool Whip®. Fold in Cool Whip® last. Put in baking cups in muffin tins and freeze. When frozen, remove from tins and store in plastic bags in freezer. Notes: Good thawed as side dish with ham at holidays or eat as is from freezer as a frozen treat. For Christmas, I use a small jar of red cherries and a small jar of green cherries. (Editor's note: If you plan to serve this frozen, crushed pineapple is recommended over tidbits.)

Nutrition facts per serving: 195 calories; 1.7 g protein; 12.4 g fat; 18.4 g carbohydrates; 0.9 g fiber; 48 mg sodium. 20 servings.

This recipe was given to me many years ago by Charlotte Blount who, for many years, reviewed children's books for the Winston-Salem Journal.
Mitzi Loflin Sapp, Friend of Clemmons Library. "Why do I love the library? Because we have the absolute greatest staff... always helpful and friendly!"

Jessica's Fruit Salad

1 ripe cantaloupe
1 apple
2 fresh peaches
2 ripe bananas
2 c. strawberries and/or grapes
20-oz. can juice-pack pineapple chunks, not drained
6-oz. can frozen orange juice concentrate, thawed

Cut fresh fruit in bite-sized pieces into large bowl. Add pineapple with juice. Pour thawed orange juice concentrate over fruit. Do not stir! Chill 6 to 8 hours. Stir and serve.

Nutrition facts per serving: 180 calories; 1.6 g protein; 16.7 g fat; 8.1 g carbohydrates; 2.6 g fiber; 166 mg sodium. 8 servings.

Jessica Cole, current staff

Orange Fruit Salad

2 20-oz. cans juice-pack pineapple chunks
2 sm. (11-oz.) cans juice-pack mandarin oranges
3 to 4 bananas, sliced
1 pkg. instant vanilla pudding
3 Tbsp. Tang® drink mix

Drain 1 can of pineapple, reserving liquid. Drain remaining canned fruit. Combine all fruit in mixing bowl. In small bowl, whisk together reserved pineapple juice, pudding mix and Tang® until well blended. Pour over fruit mixture and toss gently until all fruit is covered. Chill at least 2 hours before serving. Note: Salad can be mixed together ahead of time but add bananas just before serving to prevent them from turning dark.

Nutrition facts per serving: 141 calories; 0.7 g protein; 0.3 g fat; 34.6 g carbohydrates; 1.3 g fiber; 122 mg sodium. 12 servings.

Jennifer Wiseman, Friend of the Lewisville Library

Pineapple Delight

1 pkg. strawberry flavor gelatin
2 c. whipped cream
1 med. (15.25-oz.) can crushed juice-pack pineapple, drained
2 c. cottage cheese

Prepare gelatin according to package directions. Add remaining ingredients, stir until blended and refrigerate. When set, scoop into dish and serve.

Nutrition facts per serving: 177 calories; 8.5 g protein; 6.5 g fat; 22.5 g carbohydrates; 0 g fiber; 280 mg sodium. 8 servings.

Yvonne Rhodes, current staff

Black Bean Salsa

1 can black beans, drained and rinsed
1 can yellow corn kernels, drained
2 med. tomatoes, diced
1 red bell pepper, diced
1 green bell pepper, diced
2 to 3 fresh jalapeño or serrano peppers, sliced thin (wear gloves!)
½ c. diced red onion
1/3 c. fresh cilantro, finely chopped

Dressing

1/3 c. fresh lime juice
1/3 c. olive oil
1 tsp. salt
½ tsp. ground cumin
½ tsp. ground cayenne pepper

Combine beans, corn, tomatoes, peppers, onion and cilantro in large bowl. In separate bowl or jar, combine dressing ingredients and stir or shake until well mixed. Pour over salsa and stir to combine. Let marinate for several hours to combine flavors.

Nutrition facts per serving: 76 calories; 3.7 g protein; 0.5 g fat; 15.8 g carbohydrates; 4.8 g fiber; 458 mg sodium. 10 servings.

Served at Cooking With Herbs program, part of "Successful Gardening at the Library" series.
Janelle Kent, Extension Agent, NC Cooperative Extension Service

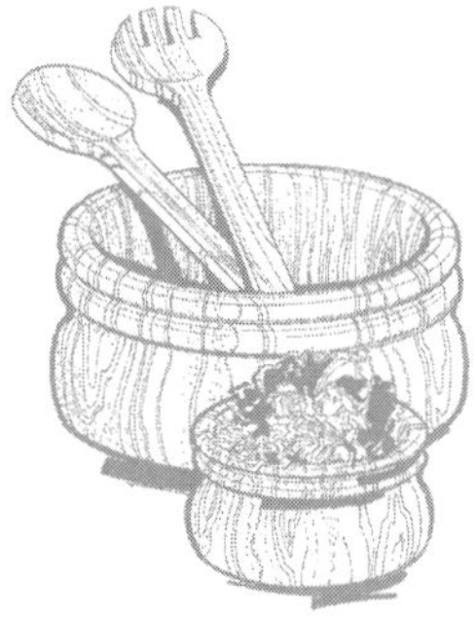

Fennel Seed Vinaigrette

3 Tbsp. white wine vinegar
1 tsp. Dijon-style prepared mustard
1 tsp. fennel seeds, crushed
½ tsp. salt
¼ tsp. fresh ground pepper
½ c. extra-virgin olive oil

In bowl, whisk together first 5 ingredients. Gradually whisk in oil. Let stand at room temperature before serving to allow flavors to blend.

Nutrition facts per serving: 163 calories; 0.1 g protein; 18.2 g fat; 0.4 g carbohydrates; 0.1 g fiber; 203 mg sodium. 6 servings.

Rob Norwood, current staff

Burgundy Bacon Vinaigrette

¼ c. red wine vinegar
2 Tbsp. Burgundy wine
¾ c. vegetable oil
pinch of salt
3 or 4 grinds of pepper mill
2 tsp. granulated sugar (or equivalent artificial sweetener)
3 or 4 drops bacon grease

Shake all ingredients together vigorously. Toss with salad of broken-up romaine, Boston, or bibb lettuce and garnish with crumbled well-cooked bacon.

Nutrition facts per serving: 126 calories; 0 g protein; 13.7 g fat; 0.9 g carbohydrates; 0 g fiber; 24 mg sodium. 8 servings.

An original recipe with a light sweet and sour flavor
Barbara Rickert, Friend of the Library

Poppy Seed Salad Dressing

1 c. granulated sugar
2 tsp. dry mustard
2 tsp. salt
⅔ c. white vinegar
3 Tbsp. grated onion
1½ c. salad oil
2 Tbsp. (or less) poppy seeds

Place the sugar, mustard, salt, vinegar and onion in blender. Blend until sugar is well mixed. Add oil slowly as it thickens. Add poppy seeds for last few seconds. Pour into jar. It will keep several weeks if refrigerated.

Nutrition facts per serving: 159 calories; 0.3 g protein; 14.0 g fat; 8.9 g carbohydrates; 0.2 g fiber; 194 mg sodium. 24 servings.

This is wonderful on a mixed veggie salad or on fruit, too. Enjoy!
This recipe was submitted anonymously

"It's certain that fine women eat
A crazy salad with their meat."

William Butler Yeats, 1865-1939
A Prayer for My Daughter

MAIN COURSES

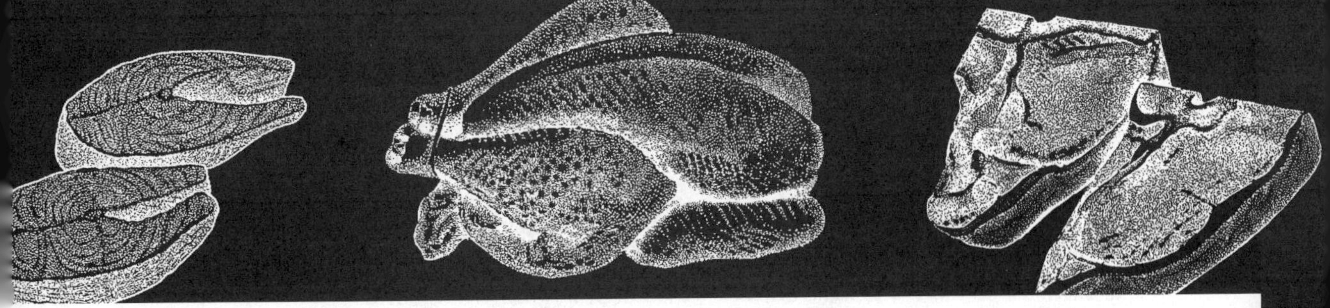

"A freeloader is a confirmed guest. He is the man who is always willing to come to dinner."

Damon Runyan, 1884-1946
Short Takes

African Chicken and Rice

5 c. rice, white or brown
5-lb. bag chicken drumettes
8 cans spinach, well drained
1 tsp. McCormick Season-All®
1 tsp. Astro® seasoning or Cajun seasoning
beef bouillon granules to taste (optional)
1/3 c. vegetable oil
pinch ground red pepper

Cook rice according to package directions. While rice is cooking, wash drumettes. Place wet drumettes in heated dry stockpot over high heat and cover. Reduce heat to medium and steam drumettes, without added water, cooking until tender. Add remaining ingredients and heat through. Serve over cooked rice. Note: You can use other meats in this dish as well: beef, turkey, etc.

Nutrition facts per serving: 383 calories; 21.5 g protein; 17.8 g fat; 34.6 g carbohydrates; 3.1 g fiber; 408 mg sodium. 20 servings.

I used to fix this for Black History Month every year. The kids loved it and would ask for more, even the ones who didn't usually like spinach!
Pat Stepney, former staff

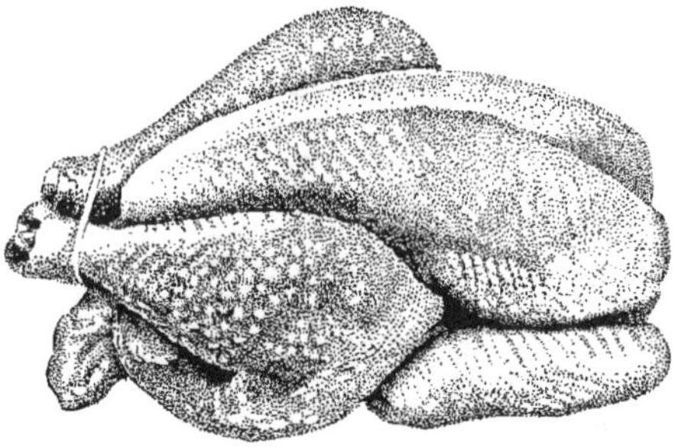

Barbecued Chicken

2½- to 3-lb. fryer chicken
salt and pepper to taste
hot water
3 onions, thinly sliced
1½ c. tomato juice
¼ tsp. cayenne pepper
2 tsp. salt
¼ tsp. ground black pepper
½ tsp. dry mustard
4½ tsp. Worcestershire sauce
1 bay leaf
1 tsp. granulated sugar
¾ c. cider vinegar
3 cloves garlic, minced
3 Tbsp. butter, margarine, or vegetable oil

Preheat oven to 350°F. Cut chicken into serving pieces and place in roasting pan. Sprinkle with salt and pepper and add hot water just to cover bottom of pan. Place sliced onions over chicken. Roast for 30 minutes, turn each piece and cook for another 30 minutes.

In large saucepan, combine all remaining ingredients. Blend and simmer for 10 minutes. When chicken has cooked for full hour (30 minutes on each side), pour off all but ¾ cup liquid. Turn pieces skin side up and pour sauce on top. Bake another hour, basting with sauce frequently.

Nutrition facts per serving: 347 calories; 28.8 g protein; 12.7 g fat; 12.4 g carbohydrates; 1.8 g fiber; 1508 mg sodium. 6 servings.

A family favorite made from scratch. The recipe came from my husband's sister when we were first married.
Donna L. Staley, Chairman of the Forsyth County Library Board of Trustees. "I love learning and the library holds the keys to learning about many varied topics."

Citrus Grilled Chicken

¼ c. lemon juice
2 Tbsp. lime juice
2 Tbsp. orange juice
1 Tbsp. olive oil
1 tsp. granulated sugar
1 tsp. dried oregano (or Italian seasoning)
1 to 1½ lb. boneless, skinless chicken breasts

Place all ingredients in zippered plastic storage bag. Place in refrigerator for at least 4 to 6 hours, turning occasionally to evenly distribute marinade. Grill chicken over medium coals for approximately 12 minutes on each side or until cooked through. Brush chicken occasionally with reserved marinade while grilling.

Nutrition facts per serving: 159 calories; 27.1 g protein; 3.4 g fat; 2.4 g carbohydrates; 0.2 g fiber; 78 mg sodium. 4 to 6 servings.

I found this recipe on a bottle of ReaLemon® lemon juice and quickly adapted it to meet my tastes. I use the leftovers as a tasty addition for a quick dinner salad.
Carole Bonnell, current staff

Miss Annie's Baked Chicken and Gravy

½ c. all-purpose flour
1 Tbsp. seasoned salt
1 tsp. ground pepper
2 tsp. garlic powder
3- to 3½-lb. frying chicken, cut into pieces
1 lg. onion, chopped
1 lg. green bell pepper, chopped
1 stick (½ c.) butter or margarine
1 sm. (5-oz.) can evaporated milk
1 can condensed cream of chicken soup

Preheat oven to 350°F. Combine flour, salt, pepper and garlic powder. Toss chicken pieces in flour mixture to coat and place in baking dish, skin side down. Bake uncovered for 40 minutes. Turn chicken skin side up and bake until brown. Sauté onion and bell pepper in butter. Combine milk, condensed soup, onions and pepper. Pour soup mixture over chicken. Cover dish with foil and return to oven. Bake 30 to 40 more minutes.

Nutrition facts per serving: 438 calories; 24.0 g protein; 31.8 g fat; 13.5 g carbohydrates; 1.1 g fiber; 1150 mg sodium. 8 servings.

Annie Johnson, former staff

Emily Williams's Swiss Chicken Casserole

1 stick (½ c.) margarine or butter, divided
1½ lb. boneless chicken breasts
8 oz. Swiss cheese
1 can condensed cream of chicken or cream of mushroom soup
8 oz. sour cream or plain nonfat yogurt
8 oz. mushrooms, sliced
4 oz. (½ sm. bag) Pepperidge Farm® stuffing, dry

Preheat oven to 325°F. Melt half of butter in 9"x13" casserole dish. Cut chicken in bite-sized pieces and arrange in butter. Slice or grate cheese and arrange over chicken. Mix soup and sour cream or yogurt and spread half of mixture over cheese. Layer mushrooms on top and spread with other half of soup mixture. Melt remaining butter and toss with stuffing. Spread on top. Bake about 1 hour. Serve with a salad, a green vegetable, a glass of white wine and some excellent literary conversation.

Nutrition facts per serving (made with sour cream): 730 calories; 45.5 g protein; 50.7 g fat; 21.3 g carbohydrates; 0.7 g fiber; 1068 mg sodium.
Per serving (made with yogurt): 664 calories; 45.8 g protein; 42.7 g fat; 22.4 g carbohydrates; 0.7 g fiber; 1070 mg sodium.
6 servings.

Emily Williams worked at FCPL for many decades of the last century. She gave me this recipe in 1987. Actually, it had twice as much butter and stuffing and didn't suggest yogurt when she fixed it.
Karen Robertson, current staff

Jazzed Up Chicken

- 1½ to 2 lb. (6 pieces) boneless chicken breast
- 16-oz. can whole cranberry sauce
- 1 pkg. dry onion soup mix
- 8 oz. French dressing

Preheat oven to 350°F. Place chicken in 9″x13″ pan or casserole dish. Mix remaining ingredients and pour over chicken. Cover with aluminum foil and bake for 40-45 minutes. Remove foil and bake for another 15-20 minutes to brown. Serve with white rice.

Nutrition facts per serving: 569 calories; 31.1 g protein; 32.1 g fat; 37.0 g carbohydrates; 1.7 g fiber; 1032 mg sodium. 6 servings.

This recipe is easy, economical and good enough for guests.
Ruth Oregar, Friend of the Lewisville Library

Karen's Mexican Chicken

- 4 chicken breasts (approx. 1 lb.)
- 1½ c. water
- 1 can condensed cream of chicken soup
- 1 can condensed cream of mushroom soup
- 1 onion, chopped
- ½ c. milk
- 10 corn tortillas
- 8 oz. salsa
- 1 sm. (7-oz.) can chopped green chilis
- 1 c. shredded Monterey jack cheese

Prepare a day before serving. Cook chicken breasts in water. Remove chicken and boil broth uncovered until reduced to about ½ cup. Chop or tear chicken into large pieces. Mix together condensed soups, onion, milk and chicken broth. Layer greased casserole dish with tortillas, salsa, green chilis, soup mixture and chicken. Refrigerate 24 hours.

Preheat oven to 350°F. Bake casserole for 45 minutes. Cover with cheese and bake 15 minutes more.

Nutrition facts per serving: 391 calories; 28.0 g protein; 16.0 g fat; 33.3 g carbohydrates; 4.6 g fiber; 1395 mg sodium. 6 servings.

Karen Robertson served this at a Public Library Quiz Bowl party years ago.
Elizabeth Skinner, current staff

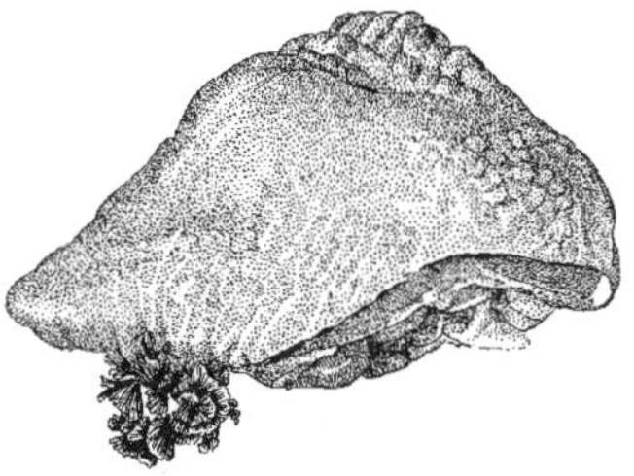

Chicken Crescents

1 lb. cooked chicken, chopped or shredded
1 c. shredded cheese, divided
22-oz. can refrigerated crescent rolls
1 can condensed cream of chicken soup
1 c. milk

Preheat oven to 375°F. Combine chicken and ½ cup cheese. Separate crescents and fill each one with chicken mixture. Roll up crescents and set aside. Combine soup, milk and remaining cheese in saucepan and heat until cheese melts. Pour half of soup mixture in 9½"x11" baking pan. Arrange stuffed crescents in pan and pour remaining soup mixture over top. Bake 15 to 20 minutes or until rolls are fully cooked.

Nutrition facts per serving: 468 calories; 24.9 g protein; 23.6 g fat; 26.3 g carbohydrates; 0.1 g fiber; 887 mg sodium. 8 servings.

Family favorite.
Teresa Floyd, current staff

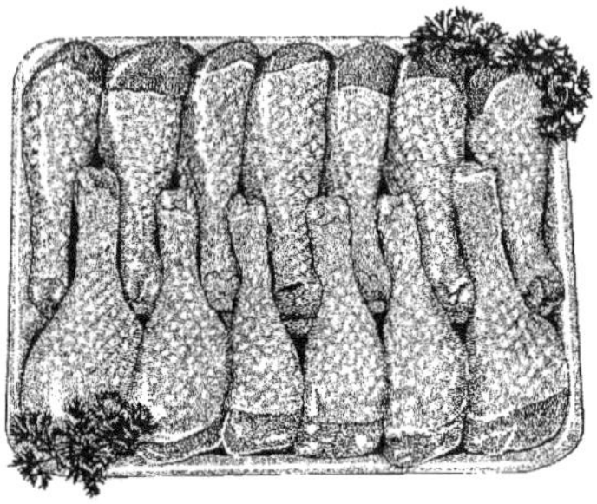

Texas Chicken Loaf

2½- to 3-lb. chicken
1½ c. milk
4 eggs
2 c. cooked rice (not instant)
2 c. toasted bread crumbs
6 Tbsp. margarine, melted
salt and pepper to taste

Boil chicken in enough water to cover. Reserve broth. Allow chicken to cool and remove bones and skin. Shred chicken into small pieces.

Preheat oven to 350°F. In large bowl, beat milk and eggs together. Add remaining ingredients and 1½ cup reserved chicken broth and mix well. Season well with salt and pepper. Pour into 9"x13" baking dish. Bake for 1 hour and 20 minutes or until firm and lightly browned. Cut in squares and serve. Note: Delicious with sauce made from 1 can of condensed cream of chicken soup and ¾ can of milk.

Nutrition facts per serving: 346 calories; 22.4 g protein; 13.2 g fat; 22.3 g carbohydrates; 0.6 g fiber; 499 mg sodium. 12 servings.

A friend in Lexington gave this recipe to me. It has become my family's favorite. I've used it at numerous church dinners. The recipe has been sent from Pennsylvania to Mississippi.
Carolene Davis, current staff. "I love to read."

Healthy Chicken Salad

3 c. cooked tri-color pasta, chilled
2 10-oz. cans white chicken
1 c. grape tomatoes
1 c. diced cucumbers (with peel)
½ c. sliced red onions
1 c. feta cheese, crumbled
1 sm. (3.25-oz.) can sliced black olives

Dressing

½ c. red wine vinegar
½ tsp. salt
1 Tbsp. fresh lemon juice
1 Tbsp. garlic powder
1 Tbsp. dried oregano

Combine pasta, chicken, vegetables, cheese and olives. Mix all dressing ingredients together, pour over pasta mixture and lightly toss until coated. Chill until ready to serve. Also good with Poppy Seed Salad Dressing (see page 24).

Nutrition facts per serving: 384 calories; 31.5 g protein; 15.5 g fat; 28.2 g carbohydrates; 3.1 g fiber; 842 mg sodium. 6 servings.

This recipe was adapted from one in a magazine.
Joan Burton, Friend of the Library. "I like the personnel at Southside. I can get bestsellers without having to buy them. My granddaughter loved the children's programs when she was small."

Lemon Blueberry Chicken Salad

2 c. fresh or frozen blueberries, divided
¾ c. low-fat lemon yogurt
3 Tbsp. light mayonnaise
1 tsp. salt
2 c. cubed cooked chicken breast
½ c. sliced green onions or scallions
¾ c. diagonally sliced celery
½ c. diced sweet red bell pepper
thin lemon slices (optional)

Reserve a few blueberries for garnish. In a medium bowl, combine yogurt, mayonnaise and salt. Add blueberries, chicken, green onions, celery and bell pepper. Mix gently. Cover and refrigerate to let flavors blend at least 30 minutes. Serve over endive or other greens. Garnish with reserved blueberries and lemon slices, if desired.

Nutrition facts per serving: 258 calories; 17.2 g protein; 8.3 g fat; 17.4 g carbohydrates; 2.1 g fiber; 631 mg sodium. 5 servings.

Delicious! A great filling for sandwiches.
Donna L. Staley, Chairman, Forsyth County Public Library Board of Trustees. "The freedom to gain knowledge through library resources is a highly prized liberty I cherish."

Hot Chicken Salad

1½ c. sliced almonds
1 Tbsp. butter
2 c. diced cooked chicken
1 c. diced celery
½ tsp. salt
½ c. mayonnaise
½ can condensed cream of mushroom soup
½ tsp. Accent® (monosodium glutamate) (optional)
2 tsp. grated onion
½ c. shredded cheddar cheese

Preheat oven to 450°F. Sauté almonds in butter. Combine drained almonds with all other ingredients and pour into baking dish. Bake for 20 minutes.

Nutrition facts per serving: 315 calories; 16.3 g protein; 21.9 g fat; 9.2 g carbohydrates; 2.4 g fiber; 522 mg sodium. 8 servings.

Alison Coward. "I served as President of the Rural Hall Friends of the Library for over 10 years. I love the library!"

"After a good dinner one can forgive anybody, even one's own relatives."

Oscar Wilde, 1854-1900
A Woman of No Importance

Rosemary Pork with Pears

1/3 c. dried cranberries or blueberries
1 Tbsp. light tub margarine
½ tsp. grated orange zest
½ tsp. ground cinnamon
1 lb. pork tenderloin
4 medium pears, halved and cored
½ tsp. dried rosemary
¼ tsp. salt
1/8 tsp. garlic powder
paprika to taste

Preheat oven to 425°F. Stir together dried fruit, margarine, orange zest and cinnamon. Lightly spray nonstick rimmed baking sheet with cooking spray. Place pork and pears with cut side up on baking sheet. Spoon berry mixture into cavity of each pear half. Sprinkle pork with rosemary, salt, garlic powder and paprika. Bake for 22 minutes or until the pork is barely pink in center (160° F. on instant-read thermometer). Transfer to cutting board and let stand for about 3 minutes. Thinly slice on diagonal.

Nutrition facts per serving: 318 calories; 25.3 g protein; 10.4 g fat; 33.4 g carbohydrates; 5.1 g fiber; 243 mg sodium. 4 servings.

Adapted from an American Heart Association recipe.
Betty Allegrone, current staff

Eastern Carolina Barbecue, the Cheater's Version

2 c. cider vinegar
2 Tbsp. crushed red pepper
1½ tsp. minced garlic
1½ tsp. cayenne pepper
1½ tsp. kosher salt
½ tsp. Texas Pete® hot sauce
1 to 2 tsp. liquid smoke, to taste (optional)
2½ -lb. pork loin roast
½ lg. onion, sliced

Mix sauce ingredients in medium bowl. Stir, cover and refrigerate overnight to allow flavors to steep. Next day, scatter onion in bottom of slow cooker or Dutch oven. Rinse meat and pat dry. Remove any strings and all visible fat and tendons. Place pork on top of onions, splitting if necessary to ensure that meat is as flat as possible. Pour half of sauce over pork, covering entire surface. Turn meat over and pour remaining sauce on other side.

For slow cooker, cover and cook on low for 8 hours. Do not lift cover until time is up! For roasting, preheat oven to 325ºF and roast in covered Dutch oven for 6 hours or until meat is ready to fall apart. Chop cooked meat coarsely or pull apart with forks. Douse with sauce from pot if you like extra flavor. For proper North Carolina presentation, serve on hamburger bun with cole slaw on top.

Nutrition facts per serving: 181 calories; 24.5 g protein; 6.7 g fat; 3.9 g carbohydrates; 0.9 g fiber; 421 mg sodium. 10 servings.

Real Eastern Carolina barbecue means roasting the whole pig ("everything but the squeal") in an oil-drum smoker using ultra-secret rubs and sauces. This is merely an approximation. Blood has been spilled in the war between Eastern and Lexington barbecue devotees, even within families (much like in The Late Unpleasantness). This Yankee and her kin are firmly in the Eastern camp.
Lise Keppler, current staff

Chopped South Carolina Barbecue

5-lb. beef roast
2-lb. pork roast
1 c. vinegar
1 onion, chopped
1 c. water
salt to taste
1 lg. (36-oz.) bottle catsup
¾ (18-oz.) bottle barbecue sauce

Place meats, vinegar, onion, water and salt in large pot. Cook slowly until tender. After shredding, place meats, catsup and barbecue sauce in slow cooker and cook on low heat for 6 to 8 hours.

Nutrition facts per serving: 267 calories; 23.9 g protein; 11.7 g fat; 14.9 g carbohydrates; 0.1 g fiber; 848 mg sodium. 28 servings.

This is a South Carolina recipe so it's got to be good!
Dot Jordan, former staff. "As a retiree, reading is my favorite pastime. I'm a fast reader so I'm a constant patron. I'll never lose my library card!"

Plantation Casserole

2 c. chopped cooked chicken, ham or beef
1 c. frozen peas
1 can cream style corn
¼ lb. American cheese, cubed
¼ c. chopped onion
1 tsp. Worcestershire sauce
1 c. dry biscuit mix
½ c. cornmeal
½ c. evaporated milk
2 tsp. sugar
½ tsp. salt
1 egg, beaten

Preheat oven to 400°F. Combine meat, peas, corn, cheese, onion and Worcestershire sauce. Pour into 8"x8" baking dish and bake for 10 minutes. Combine remaining ingredients and pour batter around edges of meat mixture, leaving center uncovered. Bake 20 minutes longer. Notes: I play with this recipe a lot. You may want to place a sheet pan underneath to catch drips.

Nutrition facts per serving (made with chicken): 341 calories; 19.4 g protein; 12.9 g fat; 29.9 g carbohydrates; 2.2 g fiber; 842 mg sodium.
Per serving (made with ham): 311 calories; 14.7 g protein; 14.6 g fat; 29.9 g carbohydrates; 2.2 g fiber; 1109 mg sodium.
Per serving (made with beef): 373 calories; 20.2 g protein; 18.9 g fat; 29.9 g carbohydrates; 2.2 g fiber; 839 mg sodium.
8 servings.

Sylvia Hauser Thompson, former staff

Down Home Ham and Potato Casserole

4 lg. potatoes, peeled and sliced approx. ¼" thick
1 can condensed cream of mushroom soup
½ tsp. salt
1 tsp. ground pepper
½ stick (4 Tbsp.) butter
½ c. milk
4 c. cooked ham, cubed
1 c. chopped onion
½ green bell pepper, chopped
½ stalk celery, chopped

Boil potatoes in salted water until done. Drain and set aside. Preheat oven to 400°F. In saucepan, combine soup, salt, pepper, butter and milk. Heat on medium until simmering, stirring to prevent sticking. Remove pan from heat. Arrange potatoes in buttered casserole dish. Layer with ham, onion, green pepper and celery. Pour soup mixture on top. Bake for 30 minutes.

Nutrition facts per serving: 374 calories; 16.2 g protein; 17.8 g fat; 38.2 g carbohydrates; 4.8 g fiber; 1083 mg sodium. 8 servings.

Brenda McCloud, current staff

Jennifer's Meatloaf

1½ lb. ground chuck
1½ c. quick-cooking (not instant) oatmeal
1 pkg. dry onion soup mix
8-oz. can tomato sauce
1 egg, beaten
2 Tbsp. Worcestershire sauce
salt and pepper to taste
2 Tbsp. brown sugar
4 Tbsp. catsup

Preheat oven to 350°F. Mix together all ingredients except brown sugar and catsup. Shape into loaf in 9"x5"x3" loaf pan. Combine brown sugar and catsup and spread over top of meatloaf. Bake for 50 minutes.

Nutrition facts per serving: 333 calories; 16.3 g protein; 22.6 g fat; 15.4 g carbohydrates; 1.8 g fiber; 784 mg sodium. 8 servings.

Jennifer Wiseman, Friend of the Lewisville Library

Decca's Combined Family Meatloaf

1½ lbs. lean ground beef or ground chuck
1 egg
seasoned salt to taste
1½ c. Heinz® catsup, divided
1 Tbsp. Worcestershire sauce
1 small onion, chopped
½ large green bell pepper, chopped
1 c. bread crumbs

Preheat oven to 350°F. In large bowl, combine ground beef, egg, seasoned salt and 1 cup catsup. Mix together lightly. Add Worcestershire sauce, onion and green pepper. Mix lightly again. Add bread crumbs and mix again. Spray loaf pan with non-stick cooking spray. Place meatloaf in pan. Bake for 45 minutes. Remove meatloaf from oven. Drizzle remaining catsup over top of meatloaf. Bake for 20 minutes more.

Nutrition facts per serving: 301 calories; 19.2 g protein; 14.3 g fat; 24.3 g carbohydrates; 1.4 g fiber; 910 mg sodium. 8 servings.

I grew up in a family where both my mother AND father love to cook. They each have very different and distinctive meatloaf recipes. Unfortunately, I did not naturally inherit their love of cooking. I am not known as the "cook" of the family. Instead I like to EAT the food everyone else cooks! However, I love meatloaf and decided one day to combine the ingredients that I liked best from each of their original recipes and make my "own" meatloaf. Both of my parents have eaten my meatloaf and my mom even asked me for the recipe once. I explained what I had done. She said that it was one of the best meatloafs she'd ever tasted and that I had indeed made it my own. The above recipe is my "combined" creation.
Decca Riedel, current staff

Sweet and Sour Meatballs

1½ lb. lean ground beef
2 eggs
½ c. dry breadcrumbs, finely crushed
1 Tbsp. Worcestershire sauce
4 tsp. beef flavor bouillon granules

Sauce

1 c. water
½ c. firmly packed light brown sugar
½ c. bottled lemon juice
¼ c. catsup
1 lg. green pepper, diced
20-oz. can juice-pack pineapple chunks, drained

In large bowl, combine meat, eggs, breadcrumbs, Worcestershire and bouillon and mix well. Shape into 1¼" meatballs. In large skillet, brown meatballs. Remove from pan and pour off fat. In same skillet, combine sauce ingredients except green pepper and pineapple. Mix well and cook over medium heat until sauce thickens. Reduce heat, add meatballs and simmer uncovered for 10 minutes. Add green pepper and pineapple and heat through.

Nutrition facts per serving: 342 calories; 18.9 g protein; 14.4 g fat; 33.4 g carbohydrates; 0.6 g fiber; 680 mg sodium. 8 servings.

This is a great party food and my family enjoys the sauce for dipping chicken nuggets.
Louis Willard, volunteer at Rural Hall Library

Carmola Quick Spaghetti

1½ lbs. lean ground beef
2 cloves garlic, minced
28-oz. can diced tomatoes
28-oz. can tomato sauce
12-oz. can V8® vegetable juice
3 7-oz. jars button mushrooms
1 pkg. McCormick® spaghetti sauce mix
1½ c. red wine (Chianti, merlot, cabernet sauvignon, etc.)
1 box (1 lb.) capellini (angel hair pasta)

Brown beef and garlic over medium to medium-high heat and drain. Add tomatoes, tomato sauce, V8®, mushrooms, sauce mix and wine. Simmer over medium heat for 30 minutes, stirring occasionally. Cook pasta according to package directions. Serve sauce over pasta with freshly grated Parmesano-Reggiano cheese and crusty French bread.

Nutrition facts per serving: 706 calories; 36.6 g protein; 19.1 g fat; 88.1 g carbohydrates; 9.2 g fiber; 1458 mg sodium. 6 servings.

Allison Carmola, current staff

Barrett Family Spaghetti and Meatballs

Sauce

3 Tbsp. olive oil
¾ c. chopped onion
1 clove garlic, minced (or ¼ tsp. from jar)
2 cans tomatoes (petite diced or puréed or a combination)
2 6-oz. cans tomato paste
1 c. water
1 Tbsp. granulated sugar
1½ tsp. salt
1 tsp. ground pepper
1½ tsp. crushed oregano
½ tsp. crushed basil (optional)
1 bay leaf

Meatballs

4 slices bread, air dried for a few hours or until bread is hard
1 lb. lean ground beef
2 eggs
½ c. grated Romano cheese
2 Tbsp. chopped parsley
1 clove garlic, minced
1 tsp. crushed oregano
1 tsp. salt
dash of ground pepper
6 Tbsp. olive oil

12 oz. dry spaghetti

To make sauce, heat olive oil in medium pot. On medium heat, cook onion and garlic in oil until onions become somewhat translucent but not brown. Stir in remaining sauce ingredients. Simmer uncovered for 30 minutes. Remove bay leaf.

To make meatballs, soak dried bread in water for about a minute, then squeeze out moisture. Combine soaked bread with remaining meatball ingredients except oil and mix lightly, using your hands. Pinch off small amounts and roll into balls (about 1" to 1¼" in diameter). Heat olive oil in frying pan and brown meatballs slowly in batches. Meatballs should cook in about 7 minutes. Do not crowd pan. As you remove batch, put them on plate with paper towels to drain. When all meatballs are cooked, add them to sauce and cook for 30 more minutes. Cook spaghetti according to package directions, drain and serve with meatballs and sauce on top.

Nutrition facts per serving: 743 calories; 30.8 g protein; 38.9 g fat; 73.1 g carbohydrates; 7.6 g fiber; 1908 mg sodium. 6 servings.

Jenny Barrett, current staff

Robert's Lasagna

2 Tbsp. + 1 tsp. olive oil, divided
1 chopped onion
1 clove garlic, minced
1 green pepper, chopped
12 to 16 sliced mushrooms, divided
1 can tomatoes
1 tsp. salt
pinch oregano
¼ tsp. crushed black peppercorns
2 tsp. chopped fresh parsley
1 lb. lean ground beef
8 oz. dry lasagna noodles
½ lb. ricotta cheese
4 oz. shredded mozzarella cheese
1 c. grated Parmesan cheese

Sauté onion, garlic, green pepper and half of mushrooms lightly in 2 Tbsp. olive oil. Add tomatoes, salt, oregano, peppercorns and parsley and stir well. Cook slowly for 10 minutes, stirring occasionally. In large pan, lightly brown ground beef and remaining sliced mushrooms in 1 tsp. olive oil. Add tomato sauce and cook for 15 minutes. Meanwhile, cook lasagna noodles according to package directions.

Preheat oven to 350°F. In bottom of casserole dish, spread layer of sauce followed by layer of cooked lasagna noodles, ricotta, mozzarella, more sauce, etc. (Do not have lasagna noodles as top layer.) Top with grated Parmesan cheese. Bake for 30 to 40 minutes.

Nutrition facts per serving: 421 calories; 25.5 g protein; 24.2 g fat; 28.3 g carbohydrates; 2.2 g fiber; 661 mg sodium. 8 servings.

Robert Burgin, former staff and current president, North Carolina Library Association

Johnny Brazili

1½ lb. lean ground beef
2 Tbsp. vegetable oil
2 med. onions, chopped
2 green peppers, chopped
1 can condensed tomato soup
1 can condensed cream of
mushroom soup
½ c. water (to rinse soup cans)
¾ tsp. salt
½ lb. Velveeta® processed cheese
2 Tbsp. Worcestershire sauce
4 oz. dry noodles or macaroni

Sear meat in oil in electric skillet. Add chopped onion and brown slightly. Add peppers, soups, water and salt and cook 20 minutes. Grate cheese. Add cheese and Worcestershire sauce to meat mixture and cook 20 minutes longer, stirring until cheese melts. Cook noodles in salted water for 10 minutes. Drain and add to meat mixture. Refrigerate for 24 hours until flavor develops fully. Reheat and serve.

Nutrition facts per serving: 447 calories; 25.6 g protein; 27.2 g fat; 25.2 g carbohydrates; 1.8 g fiber; 1132 mg sodium. 8 servings.

Barbara Rickert, Friend of Reynolda Library

Asian Salmon

½ c. chopped scallions
2" fresh ginger root, peeled and finely grated
¼ c. extra-virgin olive oil
3 Tbsp. light soy sauce
1 to 1½ lb. salmon filet

Mix first 4 ingredients. Pour over salmon. Broil for 8 to 10 minutes or until scallions are lightly browned. (We let it go until it starts to smoke.) Then lower pan to about mid-oven and lower temperature to 350°F. Bake for 8 to 10 minutes or until done. Do not overcook.

Nutrition facts per serving: 294 calories; 24.6 g protein; 21.0 g fat; 0.3 g carbohydrates; 0 g fiber; 371 mg sodium. 6 servings.

My husband Jeff gets the credit for this recipe.
Mary McAfee, current staff

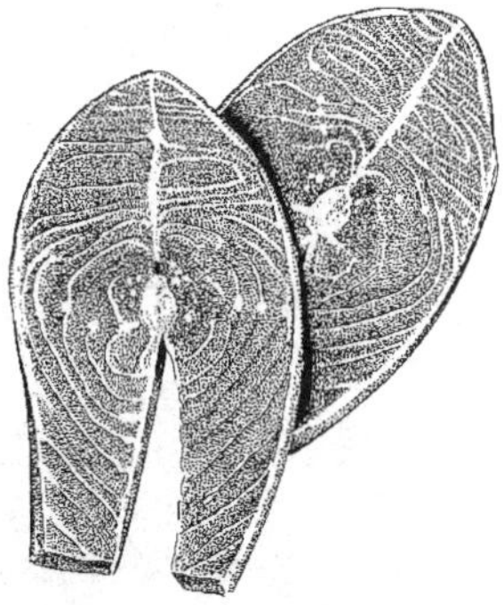

Shrimp Jambalaya

1 Tbsp. vegetable oil
1 Tbsp. all-purpose flour
1 c. chopped onion
1 c. chopped celery
1 c. chopped green bell pepper
¼ lb. lean low-salt ham, diced
2 cloves garlic, minced
2½ c. low-sodium chicken broth
¼ c. chopped fresh parsley
1 tsp. dried thyme
½ tsp. salt
½ tsp. dried basil
¼ tsp. ground black pepper
1/8 tsp. ground red pepper
1 can no-salt-added whole tomatoes, not drained, chopped
1 c. long-grain white rice, uncooked
½ lb. med. shrimp, peeled and deveined

Heat large nonstick skillet, add oil and stir in flour. Cook over medium-high heat 1½ minutes or until brown, stirring constantly. Add onion and next 4 ingredients. Sauté until tender, about 7 minutes. Add broth and next 7 ingredients, stir well and bring to boil. Add rice, stir well. Cover, reduce heat and simmer 20 minutes or until rice is tender. Stir in shrimp. Cover and cook 5 minutes or until shrimp is done.

Nutrition facts per serving: 356 calories; 19.7 g protein; 6.4 g fat; 53.1 g carbohydrates; 2.7 g fiber; 625 mg sodium. 4 servings.

Elizabeth Skinner, current staff

> "Why does Sea World have a seafood restaurant?? I'm halfway through my fish burger and I realize, Oh my God...I could be eating a slow learner."
>
> Lyndon B. Johnson, 1908-1973

Stir-Fried Shrimp and Snow Peas

1¼ lb. large shrimp, peeled and deveined
2 tsp. Chinese five-spice powder
3 Tbsp. canola or olive oil
½ lb. snow peas, halved if large
1 Tbsp. rice wine vinegar
1 Tbsp. soy sauce
¼ c. thinly sliced green onions

Sprinkle shrimp with five-spice powder. In large skillet or wok, heat oil over medium-high heat. Stir-fry shrimp just until they turn pink, 2 to 3 minutes. Add snow peas and stir-fry until crisp-tender, about 1 minute. Add vinegar, soy sauce and green onions. Simmer for about 30 seconds. Serve with steamed rice.

Nutrition facts per serving: 259 calories; 32.1 g protein; 12.4 g fat; 4.4 g carbohydrates; 1.8 g fiber; 586 mg sodium. 4 servings.

Adapted from A Flash in the Pan *by Brooke Dojny.*
Betty Allegrone, current staff

Georgia Shrimp Bake

1 stick (½ c.) butter, melted
½ c. lemon juice
½ c. Worcestershire sauce
1 Tbsp. salt
1 Tbsp. coarsely ground black pepper
1/8 tsp. ground red pepper
1 Tbsp. hot pepper sauce
3 cloves garlic, minced
2 lb. peeled large shrimp
2 lemons, thinly sliced
1 med. Vidalia onion, thinly sliced

Preheat oven to 400°F. Combine first 8 ingredients in small bowl and set aside. Rinse shrimp with cold water and drain well. Layer shrimp, lemon slices and onion slices in ungreased 9"x13" baking dish. Pour butter mixture over shrimp. Bake uncovered for 20 to 25 minutes or until shrimp turn pink, basting occasionally with pan juices. Serve with crusty French bread for dipping into sauce.

Nutrition facts per serving: 245 calories; 24.6 g protein; 12.8 g fat; 9.5 g carbohydrates; 2.1 g fiber; 1473 mg sodium. 8 servings.

Julie Walker, former staff and current PINES Program Director, Georgia Public Library Service

Seven Seas Casserole

1 can condensed cream of mushroom soup
1 can water
minced onion to taste
lemon juice to taste
1 pkg. frozen peas
1⅓ c. Minute® rice, uncooked
6-oz. can tuna, drained
½ c. bread crumbs (optional)
½ c. shredded cheese (optional)

Preheat oven to 350ºF. Dilute soup with water and heat. Add minced onion and lemon juice while cooking. At same time, cook peas according to package directions and drain. Pour half of soup mixture into bottom of greased casserole dish, then add layers of tuna, rice (straight from box) and peas. Pour rest of soup mixture on top. May be topped with bread crumbs and/or shredded cheese. Bake for 15 to 20 minutes.

Nutrition facts per serving (without bread crumbs/cheese): 413 calories; 20.1 g protein; 6.9 g fat; 65.8 g carbohydrates; 5.2 g fiber; 715 mg sodium.
Per serving (with bread crumbs/cheese): 524 calories; 25.4 g protein; 12.2 g fat; 75.7 g carbohydrates; 5.5 g fiber; 919 mg sodium.
4 servings.

Elizabeth Hull, former staff

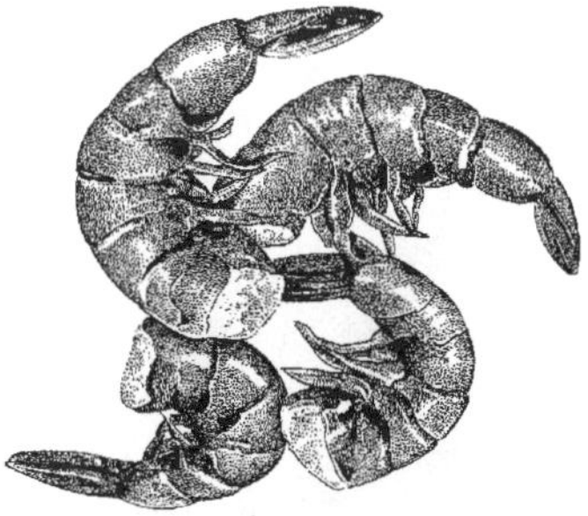

Spicy Tuna Croquettes

2 6-oz. cans water-pack tuna, drained
1 egg
4 Tbsp. all-purpose flour
½ c. diced onion
½ c. diced green bell pepper
1 Tbsp. garlic powder
1 Tbsp. dried parsley
½ tsp. salt
½ tsp. ground pepper
5 to 10 drops Texas Pete® hot pepper sauce
1 c. all-purpose flour
1 c. cornmeal
2 Tbsp. paprika
oil for frying

Combine first 10 ingredients in bowl, stir until blended and refrigerate. Combine flour, cornmeal and paprika in flat pan and blend with fork. Using large spoon, scoop tuna mixture into 1½" balls. Place croquettes in flour/cornmeal mixture and roll until coated. Heat oil in frying pan. With hands coated in flour/cornmeal mixture, pat each croquette gently into patty shape and place in hot oil. Do not crowd pan! Fry until golden brown on both sides. Drain croquettes on paper towels.

Nutrition facts per serving: 406 calories; 19.3 g protein; 20.2 g fat; 36.0 g carbohydrates; 2.6 g fiber; 409 mg sodium. 6 servings.

Rhonda B. Scales, current staff

Barrett Family Macaroni and Cheese

2 c. dry macaroni, any shape
3 Tbsp. butter
3 Tbsp. all-purpose flour
2 c. milk
2 c. grated sharp cheddar cheese
¼ c. grated muenster cheese
salt to taste

Preheat oven to 350°F. Cook macaroni according to package directions and drain. Pour pasta into 9″x9″ pan and set aside. Melt butter in saucepan over medium heat. Add flour and stir well. Add milk and stir continuously until sauce starts to thicken (approximately 5 to 7 minutes). Slowly add cheeses and stir again until all ingredients are well combined. Season as desired. Pour sauce over macaroni and fold together until well mixed. Bake for 45 minutes.

Nutrition facts per serving: 303 calories; 13.7 g protein; 21.4 g fat; 13.7 g carbohydrates; 0.4 g fiber; 528 mg sodium. 6 servings.

Jenny Barrett, current staff

Homestyle Four-Cheese Macaroni

8 oz. dry elbow macaroni
1 tsp. salt or Lowry's® seasoned salt
1 tsp. ground pepper
½ tsp. paprika
1 c. sharp cheddar cheese, shredded
1 c. provolone cheese, shredded
1 c. mozzarella cheese, shredded
1 c. colby-Monterey jack cheese, shredded
2 eggs, beaten
1 c. 2% milk

Preheat oven to 350°F. Cook macaroni in lightly salted water for 8 to 10 minutes or until done. Drain. Add salt, pepper and paprika. Spread cheddar cheese over bottom of lightly greased 8″x 8″ baking dish. Top with ⅓ of cooked macaroni. Add layer of provolone followed by ⅓ of macaroni. Add layer of mozzarella followed by remaining macaroni. Top with layer of colby-Monterey jack cheese. Beat eggs and add milk. Pour egg/milk mixture over casserole. Bake for 20 to 30 minutes or until golden brown.

Nutrition facts per serving: 353 calories; 20.7 g protein; 18.5 g fat; 25.4 g carbohydrates; 1.1 g fiber; 684 mg sodium. 8 servings.

Yolanda Bolden, current staff

Noodles and Broccoli with Saffron

¼ c. olive oil
pinch of hot pepper flakes
4 cloves garlic, minced
handful (approx. ¼ c.) dried black currants, soaked in hot water to soften then drained
handful (approx. ¼ c.) toasted pine nuts
1 small (3.25-oz.) can sliced black olives, drained
2 cups chopped canned tomatoes or tomato sauce
salt and pepper to taste
2 bunches broccoli
¼ to 1 tsp. saffron threads (the higher the quality, the less you need)
1 lb. dry noodles, any shape
¼ to ½ c. grated cheeses (Romano and Parmesan work well)

In large pot, stir-fry pepper flakes and garlic in olive oil for about 1 minute. Add currants, pine nuts, olives, tomatoes and salt and pepper. Cover and simmer for about 10 minutes. Meanwhile, wash broccoli and break into florets. Remove or trim rough stems. After first mixture has cooked, add broccoli and saffron, stir and place lid on again. Cook for 15 minutes.

While broccoli is cooking, boil noodles in salted water. (No oil! It keeps noodles from absorbing flavor later). Drain and quickly rinse noodles when finished cooking. Add cooked noodles to pot of broccoli and sauce. Toss gently and adjust seasoning if necessary. Sprinkle with half of cheese, stir together and transfer to warmed serving dish. Cover with remaining cheese and serve immediately.

Nutrition facts per serving: 534 calories; 20.2 g protein; 20.6 g fat; 72.5 g carbohydrates; 10.6 g fiber; 603 mg sodium. 6 servings.

Adapted from Lorenza's Pasta *by Lorenza de'Medici*
Andrea Morgan, wife of current staff member Ben Morgan

"Sir Christopher Wren
Said 'I am going to dine with some men.
If anybody calls
Say I am designing St. Paul's'."

Edmund Clerihew Bentley, 1875-1956
Sir Christopher Wren

Herbed Lentils and Rice

¾ c. dry lentils
¾ c. onion, chopped
½ c. uncooked brown rice
½ tsp. dried basil, crushed
¼ tsp. dried oregano, crushed
¼ tsp. dried thyme, crushed
1/8 tsp. garlic powder
1/8 tsp. ground pepper
2 2/3 c. broth (chicken or vegetable)
¼ c. dry white wine
4 oz. Swiss cheese

Preheat oven to 350ºF. Combine first 8 ingredients. Add broth and wine and mix well. Shred half of cheese and stir into lentil mixture. Turn into greased 1½-quart casserole. Cover and bake for 1½ to 2 hours, stirring twice, until lentils and rice are done. Cut remaining cheese into strips. Top casserole with cheese and bake uncovered until cheese strips melt.

Nutrition facts per serving: 271 calories; 19.8 g protein; 8.4 g fat; 26.7 g carbohydrates; 11.8 g fiber; 448 mg sodium. 4 servings.

This recipe came from a tiny almost-vegetarian with boundless energy. Must have been the lentils that made her so perky!
Lise Keppler, current staff

Three-Pepper Linguine

2 Tbsp. olive oil
1 large green bell pepper, coarsely chopped
1 large red bell pepper, coarsely chopped
1 large yellow bell pepper, coarsely chopped
½ onion, chopped
2 garlic cloves, minced
1 c. canned Italian-style plum tomatoes, drained and chopped
8 ounces spinach linguine, freshly cooked
½ c. prepared pesto
¼ c. grated Parmesan

Heat oil in heavy large skillet over medium heat. Add peppers, onion and garlic and sauté about 6 minutes. Stir in tomatoes and simmer about 7 minutes. Toss the linguine with the pesto and divide evenly among 4 plates. Spoon sauce over linquine and sprinkle with Parmesan.

Nutrition facts per serving: 487 calories; 13.1 g protein; 20.7 g fat; 64.1 g carbohydrates; 5.5 g fiber; 540 mg sodium. 4 servings.

Adapted from Bon Appetit, September 1990
Betty Allegrone, current staff

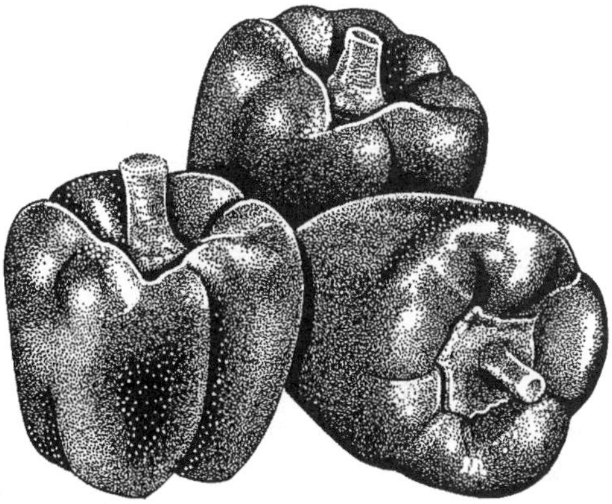

Stuffed Peppers

4 green, yellow or red bell peppers
water
½ c. pine nuts
2 Tbsp. olive oil
2 sm. onions, grated
1 c. cooked white rice, packed
½ c. currants
½ tsp. salt, or to taste
½ tsp. pepper, or to taste
chopped fresh parsley and dill to taste

Cut off tops of bell peppers, discarding stems, seeds and membranes. Chop remainder of pepper tops and set aside. Steam peppers in 1″ of boiling water for 10 minutes or until just slightly soft, then drain upside down on towel. Toast pine nuts in dry non-stick skillet on medium heat until golden brown, stirring constantly to prevent scorching. Remove nuts from pan, return pan to heat and add olive oil. When oil is hot, add onions and chopped pepper tops. Cook until softened and slightly translucent. Turn off heat and add cooked rice, currants, salt, pepper and pine nuts, stirring to mix. Add parsley and dill if desired. Spoon mixture into cooked peppers, chill and serve. (Editor's note: Peppers may also be reheated in microwave or traditional oven and served warm.)

Nutrition facts per serving: 349 calories; 6.0 g protein; 18.5 g fat; 44.1 g carbohydrates; 5.0 g fiber; 297 mg sodium. 4 servings.

Nancy Belchee, former staff

Roasted Beans with Garlic and Olives

- 3 Tbsp. extra-virgin olive oil
- 1-lb. pkg. frozen lima beans
- 6 large cloves garlic, peeled and halved or quartered length-wise
- 1 heaping c. green olives, pitted and sliced, with juice (I usually get smaller olives and don't bother cutting them)
- 1 to 2 Tbsp. crushed thyme
- 1 to 2 Tbsp. rubbed sage
- salt and pepper to taste

Preheat oven to 375°F. Mix all ingredients together (beans are frozen) and bake for 50 minutes, covered tightly, or until garlic is tender. Drizzle more olive oil or olive juice and add more salt and/or pepper if needed. Serve hot, warm, or room temperature. Note: Serve with rice as main dish, or can be served by itself in smaller portions as side dish.

Nutrition facts per serving: 607 calories; 9.8 g protein; 17.0 g fat; 30.3 g carbohydrates; 7.8 g fiber; 1430 mg sodium. 4 servings.

Andrea Morgan, wife of current staff member Ben Morgan

SOUPS & STEWS

Best Ever Crock-Pot® Stew

3 to 5 raw potatoes, peeled and cubed
seasoned salt or salt and pepper to taste
1 lb. baby carrots, peeled
1 med. onion, quartered
1 lb. lean stew beef, rinsed
1 cube beef bouillon (optional)
1 can condensed cream of mushroom soup
1 can condensed tomato soup
1 can green peas

Spray inside of Crock-Pot® (or other slow cooker) with cooking spray. Place potato pieces into pot and sprinkle with seasoned salt or salt and pepper. Add carrots and onion to pot. Add beef and bouillon cube and season again. Pour undiluted cream of mushroom soup over beef. Do not stir, just leave soup on top. Pour undiluted tomato soup over mushroom soup. Again, do not stir. Place lid on pot and cook on low heat for 8 to 10 hours. One hour before serving, drain peas and add to pot. No need to stir. Replace lid and continue cooking on low for last hour. Stir stew gently before serving. Serve with cornbread, garlic or cheese toast, biscuits, or other bread. This is a complete meal in itself—just add a salad if desired.

Nutrition facts per serving: 460 calories; 22.9 g protein; 16.9 g fat; 55.5 g carbohydrates; 8.0 g fiber; 1395 mg sodium. 6 servings.

My sister shared this recipe with me many years ago. It has been a family favorite ever since and is so easy to make when evenings are rushed with meetings, PTA, and other events or when in need of a good winter meal of comfort food. Dianne Riedel, mother of current staff member. "I have always loved the library and being surrounded by books. I took our daughters to the library as toddlers weekly to make reading and books a daily part of their lives. Our oldest daughter began working at age 16 as a page and is now Library Supervisor of one of the branch libraries."

"Anyone who tells a lie has not a pure heart and cannot make a good soup."

Ludwig Van Beethoven, 1770-1827

Five-Hour Stew

2 lb. lean stew beef, cubed
1 c. sliced celery
1 c. sliced carrots
1 c. sliced onions
½ green bell pepper, diced
3 Tbsp. all-purpose flour
1 Tbsp. salt
1 can diced tomatoes
3 Tbsp. dry sherry
1 Tbsp. granulated sugar

Toss the beef, celery, carrots, onions and green pepper with flour and salt to coat. Combine all ingredients in slow cooker and cook on high for 5 to 6 hours. Or combine all ingredients in Dutch oven, cover and bake at 300ºF for 5 hours.

Nutrition facts per serving: 306 calories; 22.8 g protein; 18.1 g fat; 10.9 g carbohydrates; 1.8 g fiber; 1029 mg sodium. 8 servings.

Bob May, former staff

Brunswick Stew

3-lb. stewing chicken
1 lb. ground beef (round steak, chuck or sirloin)
2 lg. potatoes, peeled and diced into small pieces
1 lg. onion, chopped
1 to 2 c. chicken broth
1 can chopped tomatoes
3 pkgs. frozen baby lima beans
½ c. catsup
1 Tbsp. Worcestershire sauce
1 tsp. Texas Pete® hot sauce
1 can whole kernel corn
1 can cream style corn
1 tsp. granulated sugar
salt and pepper to taste
2 Tbsp. butter

Place chicken in large pot, cover with water and simmer until tender. Cool and remove meat from bones, discarding skin. Strain broth and return to pot along with chopped chicken meat. In separate pan, brown ground beef. Drain off excess fat. Add browned beef to chicken. Add potatoes, onions, broth, tomatoes, frozen lima beans, catsup, Worcestershire sauce and hot sauce. Simmer uncovered until limas and other vegetables are tender and soup is thickened, about one hour. Add additional broth or water if needed. Finally, add corn, sugar, salt and pepper and butter. Continue simmering uncovered an additional 15 to 20 minutes more, stirring occasionally to avoid sticking. Taste for seasoning.

Nutrition facts per serving: 480 calories; 28.8 g protein; 21.3 g fat; 44.5 g carbohydrates; 7.4 g fiber; 948 mg sodium. 12 servings.

Jerry Carroll, current staff

Chicken Stew

2 lbs. chicken breast
4 Tbsp. vegetable oil
2 cans green beans
3 cans whole potatoes
1 lb. baby carrots
salt and pepper to taste
garlic salt, onion salt, or garlic powder to taste
4 Tbsp. butter, melted
1 box frozen corn kernels
6 cubes chicken bouillon
6 c. water

Cube chicken and brown in vegetable oil. Cook until moist and falling apart. Bring beans to boil in one pot and carrots and potatoes in another pot. Drain and mix all cooked ingredients in large pot. Add spices, butter, corn, bouillon and water. Cook on medium to high heat until stew is hot. Serve with bread of any kind.

Nutrition facts per serving: 362 calories; 17.3 g protein; 17.5 g fat; 30.6 g carbohydrates; 5.9 g fiber; 1901 mg sodium. 8 servings.

Paul Kwiatkowski, current staff

Spicy Chili

1½ lb. lean stew beef or ground beef
1 lg. onion, chopped
4 cloves garlic, diced
1 bell pepper, chopped
1 jalapeño pepper, diced (wear gloves!)
1 habanero pepper, diced (wear gloves!)
1 lg. (28-oz.) can whole tomatoes
8-oz. can tomato sauce
1 tsp. salt
2 Tbsp. chili powder
¼ tsp. red pepper
¼ tsp. paprika
1 can dark red kidney beans
15-oz. can pitted black olives

In large skillet, brown meat and drain fat. Remove meat and set aside. In same pan, sauté onion, garlic and peppers until soft (about 3 to 4 minutes). Put meat, sautéed vegetables, tomatoes and tomato sauce in large pot or slow cooker. Add salt and spices. If cooking on stove, bring mixture to boil, cover, reduce heat and let simmer 1½ hours. If using slow cooker, cook on low heat for 5 to 6 hours. At final half hour, add beans and olives. Note: This is a VERY spicy recipe. For additional heat, add more habaneros and spices.

Nutrition facts per serving: 348 calories; 21.0 g protein; 19.8 g fat; 24.2 g carbohydrates; 8.7 g fiber; 1150 mg sodium. 8 servings.

Art Weeks, former staff member

Vegetarian Chili, Cincinnati-Style

1 c. onions, chopped
3 large cloves garlic, chopped
2 bags Morningstar Farms® Recipe Crumbles, other brands work fine too
1 Tbsp. ground cumin
1½ tsp. oregano, crushed
1 tsp. ground cinnamon
1 tsp. ground red pepper
32 oz. tomato juice, V8® vegetable juice, or spicy V8®
28-oz. can diced tomatoes, with juice
2 6-oz. cans tomato paste
2 Tbsp. cider vinegar
2 bay leaves
28-oz. can Bush's® Vegetarian Beans, lightly drained

In Dutch oven, lightly brown onions. Add garlic and stir constantly for 2 to 3 minutes. Add crumbles, cumin, oregano, cinnamon and red pepper and continue to stir until you can really smell the spices. Add everything else except the beans and simmer for about 30 minutes. Stir in beans and heat through. Remove bay leaves. Notes: May be served plain, or do it up right and serve over vermicelli and garnish with onions and grated cheddar. Also really great with chili-cheese Fritos®!!

Nutrition facts per serving: 310 calories; 22.5 g protein; 4.3 g fat; 49.5 g carbohydrates; 11.6 g fiber; 1475 mg sodium. 8 servings.

This recipe originally called for ground turkey, but this version has much less fat and is a great source of fiber. It won a chili contest once, and I didn't even reveal that it was vegetarian!! Very easy to throw together and freezes well. The cinnamon sounds strange, but it's really good and nobody will guess the secret ingredient.
Julie James, former staff

Eggplant Supper Soup

2 Tbsp. each olive oil and butter
1 med. onion, chopped
1 lb. ground chuck
1 med. eggplant, peeled and cubed
1 clove garlic, crushed
1 c. each carrots and celery, finely sliced
2 cans whole tomatoes, broken into pieces
3½ c. beef broth
½ tsp. nutmeg
1 tsp. granulated sugar
1 tsp. salt
½ tsp. ground pepper
½ c. uncooked barley or macaroni
2 Tbsp. fresh parsley, minced

Heat oil and butter in 6- to 8-quart Dutch oven. Add onion and sauté until light brown, about 8 minutes. Add beef and brown, draining fat. Add eggplant, garlic, carrots, celery, tomatoes, broth, nutmeg, sugar, salt and pepper. Bring to boil, reduce heat, cover and simmer for 2½ hours. 10 to 15 minutes before serving, add barley or macaroni and parsley. Simmer until barley or macaroni is cooked. Optional: Garnish each serving with Parmesan cheese.

Nutrition facts per serving (made with barley): 182 calories; 9.9 g protein; 10.7 g fat; 13.4 g carbohydrates; 3.5 g fiber; 573 mg sodium.
Per serving(made with macaroni): 170 calories; 9.7 g protein; 10.6 g fat; 10.4 g carbohydrates; 2.3 g fiber; 573 mg sodium.
12 servings.

This is the perfect soup for a cold winter evening in front of a fire. It's adapted from one of my favorite recipes from the Junior League's Stirring Performances *cookbook, which was published in 1988 to raise funds for the refurbishment of the Stevens Center for the Performing Arts.*
William Durham, current staff

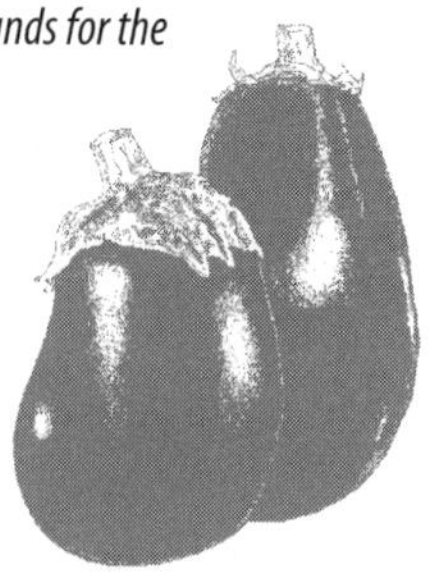

Mom's Chicken Noodle Soup

4 chicken breasts or 1 chicken cut into pieces
3 bay leaves
4 stalks celery, chopped
1 tsp. salt
1 lb. baby carrots, sliced
1 14-oz. can low-sodium chicken broth
8 oz. dry egg noodles

Remove skin from chicken and rinse. Place chicken, bay leaves, celery and salt in stock pot. Cover with water to 1" above chicken. Bring to boil and simmer for 30 minutes. Remove chicken pieces to cool. Debone chicken and cut into bite-sized pieces. Add chicken and carrots to stock. Simmer for 15 minutes. Add can of broth and egg noodles. Simmer for another 10 minutes. Serve with crusty bread and salad.

Nutrition facts per serving: 356 calories; 19.7 g protein; 6.4 g fat; 53.1 g carbohydrates; 2.7 g fiber; 625 mg sodium. 8 servings.

Elizabeth Skinner, current staff

Homemade Vegetable Beef Soup

1 lb. lean stew beef, cut in bite-sized pieces
1 lg. onion, chopped
2 c. cooked lima beans (or 1 can)
1½ c. cooked corn (or 1 box frozen kernels)
1 can diced tomatoes
salt and pepper to taste
⅓ c. cooked macaroni (optional)

Put beef and onion in Dutch oven or other pot with enough water to cover. Cook until tender. Add all vegetables. Add salt and pepper to taste. (You may wish to add more later.) Cook 1½ hours on low heat. Add cooked macaroni, if desired, for the final 30 minutes. Note: Other vegetables can be used. I have thrown in green beans and potatoes.

Nutrition facts per serving: 223 calories; 15.3 g protein; 9.2 g fat; 20.4 g carbohydrates; 4.4 g fiber; 663 mg sodium. 8 servings.

Teresa Floyd, current staff

Armenian Lentil Soup

1 c. chopped onion
½ c. each sliced carrots and sliced celery
3 c. cubed eggplant (1 med., peeled)
1 diced green pepper
3 to 6 cloves garlic, minced
3 Tbsp. olive oil
6 c. stock or low-sodium broth
1½ c. dry lentils
1½ c. chopped tomato
4 oz. dried apricots, sliced
¼ tsp. each cinnamon, allspice, and cayenne
1 Tbsp. paprika
1½ tsp. salt
3 Tbsp. fresh parsley, chopped
1 Tbsp. fresh mint, chopped

Sauté vegetables in olive oil until lightly browned. Add everything else except fresh herbs and simmer until lentils are tender. Stir in fresh herbs right before serving.

Nutrition facts per serving: 254 calories; 13.5 g protein; 6.0 g fat; 39.5 g carbohydrates; 15.1 g fiber; 872 mg sodium. 8 servings.

This recipe is wonderfully rich and exotic without being too weird. The apricots disappear, but really make a difference in the flavor! Very healthy and freezes quite well.
Julie James, former staff

Curried Pea Soup

2 to 3 leeks (1½ c. chopped)
3 Tbsp. butter
16-oz. pkg. dry green split peas, washed
8 c. water
2 carrots, chopped
1 stalk celery, chopped
½ tsp. salt (or more, to taste)
½ tsp. ground black pepper
1 or 2 Tbsp. curry powder (to taste)
½ tsp. grated fresh ginger or 1/8 tsp. powdered ginger
2 c. milk

Split leeks lengthwise and wash thoroughly. Discard roots and all green portions of leeks and coarsely chop white parts. Sauté leeks in butter in large pot until softened. Add peas and water, bring to boil, reduce heat and simmer for 2 minutes. Add carrots, celery, salt and pepper, stir and cover. Simmer until peas are very tender, about 1 hour, stirring occasionally. Add more water if necessary—do not allow peas to stick or get dry. Add curry powder and ginger and stir. In blender or food processor, carefully blend 2 cups of soup with milk until thick and silky smooth. (Use caution with hot liquids in blender. Splatters can burn!) Return blended soup to pot and stir. For very smooth soup, blend entire pot of soup using wand blender. Note: Leeks may be replaced by very mild sweet onion, such as Vidalia.

Nutrition facts per serving: 373 calories; 20.2 g protein; 10.4 g fat; 52.1 g carbohydrates; 19.2 g fiber; 349 mg sodium. 6 servings.

Adapted from Blue Moon Soup *by Gary Goss.*
Lise Keppler, current staff

Potato Cheese Soup

½ stick (¼ c.) butter
½ c. chopped onion
2 Tbsp. all-purpose flour
2 c. milk
2 c. chicken broth
2 large russet potatoes, peeled and diced
½ tsp. salt
1 c. grated sharp cheddar cheese
pepper to taste

Melt butter in heavy saucepan over medium heat. Add onion and sauté about 5 minutes. Add flour, stir and cook about 3 minutes. Gradually mix in milk and broth. Add potatoes and salt. Reduce heat and simmer until potatoes are tender, stirring occasionally, about 20 minutes. Add cheese and stir until cheese melts and soup is smooth. Garnish with extra grated cheese and freshly ground black pepper.

Nutrition facts per serving: 463 calories; 17.0 g protein; 25.9 g fat; 43.2 g carbohydrates; 4.5 g fiber; 941 mg sodium. 4 servings.

Rob Norwood, current staff

"Soup of the evening, beautiful soup!"

Lewis Carroll, 1832-1898
Alice's Adventures in Wonderland

Tuna Chowder

¼ c. sliced green onion
2 Tbsp. butter
2 cans condensed cream of potato soup
1½ c. milk
¼ c. dry white wine
1 tsp. Worcestershire sauce
¼ tsp. ground pepper
12-oz. can water-pack tuna, drained and broken into chunks

In saucepan, sauté onion in butter until tender. Add soup. Gradually stir in milk, wine, Worcestershire sauce and pepper. Add tuna and heat through.

Nutrition facts per serving: 308 calories; 26.0 g protein; 12.5 g fat; 18.9 g carbohydrates; 0.6 g fiber; 1613 mg sodium. 4 servings.

Adapted from Better Homes & Gardens Meals For One or Two
Rob Norwood, current staff

"The lore has not died out of the world, and you will find people who believe that soup will cure any hurt or illness and is no bad thing to have for the funeral either."

John Steinback, 1902-1968
East of Eden

SIDE DISHES

Broccoli Casserole

1 med. onion, coarsely chopped
1 stick (½ c.) + 1 Tbsp. butter, divided
2 pkg. frozen chopped broccoli, thawed
8 oz. cream cheese, at room temperature
1 can condensed cream of mushroom soup
1 sleeve (approx. 4 oz.) saltine crackers

Preheat oven to 350°F. Sauté onion in 1 tablespoon butter. In medium bowl, combine onion, broccoli, cream cheese and mushroom soup. Pour mixture into casserole dish. Crush crackers and mix with remaining butter. Spread over broccoli mixture. Bake for 30 minutes.

Nutrition facts per serving: 322 calories; 5.9 g protein; 26.1 g fat; 19.4 g carbohydrates; 3.4 g fiber; 698 mg sodium. 8 servings.

Judy Prater, current staff

"The only really good vegetable is Tabasco Sauce."

P. J. O'Rourke, 1947–
The Bachelor Home Companion

Broccoli Cheese Casserole

2 pkgs. frozen chopped broccoli
¾ c. mayonnaise
1 can condensed cream of mushroom soup
1 egg
1½ c. grated extra-sharp cheddar cheese
1½ c. crushed snack crackers (approx. 35 crackers), such as Waverly Wafers® or Captains Wafers®
milk

Preheat oven to 375°F. Cook broccoli according to package directions and drain. While broccoli is cooking, beat together mayonnaise, soup and egg in large bowl. Mix in drained broccoli. Then add cheese and mix. Pour into casserole dish and completely cover top with cracker crumbs. Drizzle with milk. Bake for 45 minutes. Note: For best results, prepare this a day ahead and refrigerate overnight. Before serving, bake again for another 45 minutes at 375°F.

Nutrition facts per serving: 309 calories; 9.8 g protein; 21.5 g fat; 20.4 g carbohydrates; 2.4 g fiber; 696 mg sodium. 8 servings.

This is a standard for my family's Thanksgiving dinner each year. I got this recipe from David Lee, a friend of mine from when I lived in the mountains. Cooking the full 45 minutes on both days makes it great.
Rob Norwood, current staff

Broccoli Rice Casserole

1 pkg. chopped frozen broccoli
1 sm. (8-oz.) jar Cheez Whiz® processed cheese spread
1 med. onion, chopped
½ stick (4 Tbsp.) margarine
1½ c. cooked white rice
1 can condensed cream of chicken soup

Preheat oven to 350ºF. Heat frozen broccoli in microwave for 3 to 4 minutes. Heat Cheez Whiz in microwave for 1 minute. Cook onion and margarine in microwave until tender, about 1 to 2 minutes. Put all ingredients in greased 9″x13″ pan or large casserole dish and mix. Bake for about 45 minutes or until lightly browned on top. Note: You can substitute cream of celery or cream of mushroom soup for cream of chicken.

Nutrition facts per serving: 299 calories; 7.1 g protein; 19.8 g fat; 24.4 g carbohydrates; 2.4 g fiber; 1060 mg sodium. 6 servings.

This is a recipe my mother has made for many years for our family's special meals—holidays, birthdays, etc. It is always requested for Thanksgiving and Christmas dinners.
Decca Riedel, current staff. "I began working for Forsyth County Public Library as a Library Page at the Clemmons Branch. I decided to make librarianship my career. I am now the Library Supervisor of the Southside Branch Library."

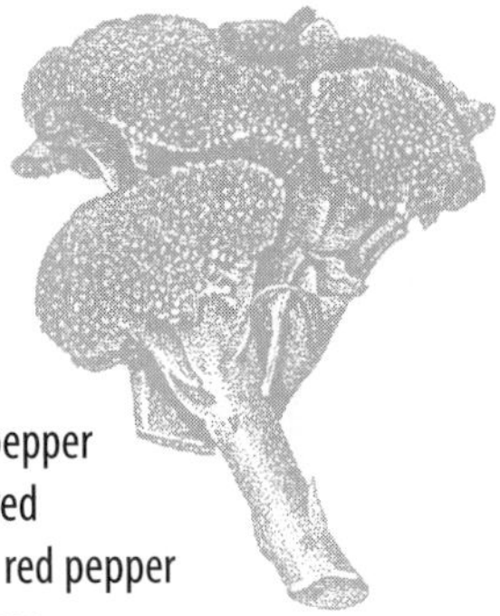

Green Bean Casserole

1 can French style green beans, drained
1 Tbsp. butter or margarine
1 Tbsp. all-purpose flour
1 c. sour cream
½ tsp. granulated sugar
½ tsp. salt
¼ tsp. ground pepper
1½ onions, grated
dash of ground red pepper
½ c. grated cheese
1 c. corn flakes, crushed

Preheat oven to 400ºF. Place green beans in 9″x9″ baking dish. In saucepan, combine and heat butter, flour, sour cream, sugar, salt, pepper and onion. Add dash of red pepper. When heated through, pour mixture over green beans. Cover with cheese and corn flakes. Bake for 20 minutes.

Nutrition facts per serving: 279 calories; 7.6 g protein; 19.7 g fat; 19.5 g carbohydrates; 3.0 g fiber; 779 mg sodium. 4 servings.

I always double this recipe for family gatherings and there are never any leftovers.
Teresa Floyd, current staff

Cheesy Mushroom Green Bean Casserole

1 c. milk
1/8 tsp. ground pepper (or more if you like)
2 cans Campbell's® Golden Mushroom condensed soup
4 cans French style green beans
6-oz. can French's® Cheddar French Fried Onions
4 c. mixed shredded cheese (I use Kraft® "Pizza" blend)
2 sm. (4-oz.) cans mushroom stems and pieces

Preheat oven to 350°F. Mix all ingredients except ¼ can French fried onions and 1 cup shredded cheese in large casserole dish. Bake for 30 minutes or until hot. Stir. Top with remaining French fried onions and shredded cheese. Bake for additional 5 minutes.

Nutrition facts per serving: 314 calories; 11.8 g protein; 22.1 g fat; 17.3 g carbohydrates; 2.8 g fiber; 1174 mg sodium. 12 servings.

Decca Riedel, current staff

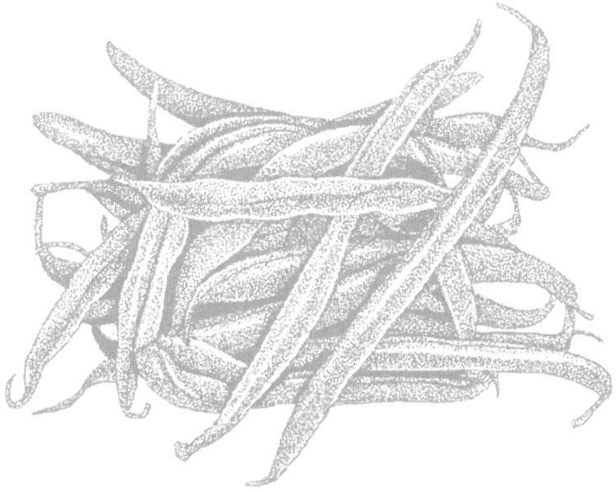

Vegetable Casserole

1 can lima beans
1 can green beans
1 can corn kernels
1 c. sour cream
1 can condensed cream of mushroom soup
1½ c. shredded cheddar cheese
1 sleeve (4 oz.) Ritz® crackers, crumbled
1 stick (½ c.) butter or margarine, melted

Preheat oven to 350°F. Drain vegetables. Mix with sour cream, soup and 1 cup shredded cheese. Place in casserole or baking dish. Top with remaining cheese, cracker crumbs and drizzle with butter or margarine. Bake approximately 40 minutes or until hot and bubbly.

Nutrition facts per serving: 436 calories; 11.9 g protein; 30.7 g fat; 29.7 g carbohydrates; 5.1 g fiber; 1027 mg sodium. 8 servings.

Adapted from the Bob Timberlake© cookbook, Recipes From Home. *It's very quick and easy to make. Also very good.*
Mae K. Redfield, Friend of Lewisville Library

Tomato Pie

unbaked 9" pie shell
3 med. tomatoes, sliced
salt and pepper to taste
¼ c. chopped spring onions
½ tsp. dried basil
¼ tsp. garlic powder
1 c. shredded cheddar cheese
½ c. mayonnaise

Preheat oven to 350°F. Line pie crust with sliced tomatoes, overlapping as needed. Season with salt and pepper. Sprinkle with onions, basil and garlic powder. Combine cheese and mayonnaise and spread on top. Bake for 30 minutes.

Nutrition facts per serving: 239 calories; 4.2 g protein; 16.6 g fat; 18.3 g carbohydrates; 1.2 g fiber; 532 mg sodium. 6 servings.

Teresa Floyd, current staff

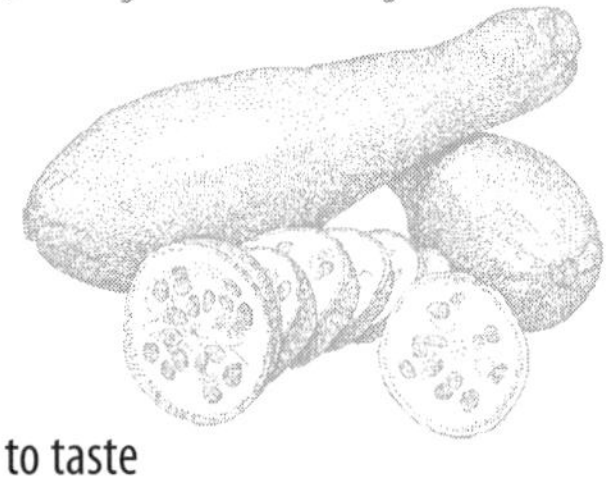

Squash and Cheese Casserole

2 c. cooked summer squash
½ stick (4 Tbsp.) margarine, melted
1 sm. onion, chopped
½ c. milk
1 egg, beaten
salt and pepper to taste
1 c. Ritz® cracker crumbs
1 c. grated cheese

Preheat oven to 350°F. Combine all ingredients except cheese. Pour into buttered casserole dish. Top with cheese and bake for 40 minutes or until bubbly.

Nutrition facts per serving: 245 calories; 8.3 g protein; 16.9 g fat; 16.0 g carbohydrates; 1.6 g fiber; 551 mg sodium. 6 servings.

Teresa Floyd, current staff

Squash Casserole

2 c. cooked summer squash, mashed
  and drained
¼ c. chopped onion
1 can cream of chicken soup
1 stick (½ c.) margarine
8-oz. pkg. herb dry stuffing mix, divided

Preheat oven to 350°F. Mix squash, onion, soup, ¾ of margarine and half of stuffing mix. Pour into baking dish and top with remaining stuffing mix. Dot with remaining margarine on top. Bake for 30 minutes.

Nutrition facts per serving: 343 calories; 6.5 g protein; 19.8 g fat; 36.0 g carbohydrates; 2.3 g fiber; 1320 mg sodium. 6 servings.

Decca Riedel, current staff

Sweet Potato Casserole

3 c. cooked sweet potatoes
1 c. granulated sugar
½ tsp. salt
1 stick (½ c.) margarine or butter, softened
½ c. milk
2 eggs
1 tsp. vanilla extract
1 tsp. cinnamon

Topping

1 c. packed brown sugar
1/3 c. all-purpose flour
1/3 stick (2 Tbsp. and 2 tsp.) margarine or butter
1 c. chopped pecans

Preheat oven to 350ºF. Mash sweet potatoes. Add remaining casserole ingredients and mix well. Pour into greased casserole dish. Using pastry blender, combine all topping ingredients. Spread topping over casserole. Bake for 30 to 35 minutes.

Nutrition facts per serving: 550 calories; 5.4 g protein; 27.5 g fat; 74.2 g carbohydrates; 4.2 g fiber; 368 mg sodium. 8 servings.

Vicki Taylor, current staff

Roasted Sweet Potato Wedges

2 8-oz. sweet potatoes, peeled
1 Tbsp. olive oil
½ tsp. curry powder
¼ tsp. salt
¼ tsp. ground cumin
1/8 tsp. ground cloves
1/8 tsp. ground pepper

Preheat oven to 425ºF. Cut sweet potatoes in half lengthwise. Cut each half lengthwise into 6 wedges. Combine potatoes and remaining ingredients in a bowl and toss gently to coat. Place wedges on baking sheet without overlapping. Bake for 25 to 30 minutes or until very tender, turning half way through.

Nutrition facts per serving: 142 calories; 1.3 g protein; 7.1 g fat; 20.9 g carbohydrates; 2.6 g fiber; 174 mg sodium. 4 servings.

Carolyn Price, current staff

"Money is the root of all evil, and yet it is such a useful root that we cannot get on without it any more than we can without potatoes."

Louisa May Alcott, 1832-1888

Roasted Vegetables

½ lb. carrots, peeled and cut 2" long
(or use baby carrots)
3/4 lb. fresh green beans, trimmed
1 large onion
1 red pepper
2 Tbsp. garlic, minced
¼ c. olive oil
1½ tsp. Italian seasoning
salt and pepper to taste
2 Tbsp. balsamic vinegar (optional)

Preheat oven to 450°F. Spray large roasting pan with cooking spray. Place carrots and green beans in pan. Peel onion, cut in half, cut halves in crescent shapes about ¼" and add to pan. Rinse pepper, cut in half and discard stem, seeds and membranes. Cut into ¼" strips and add to pan. Sprinkle garlic, olive oil, Italian seasoning, salt and pepper on vegetables. Stir and toss until vegetables are coated with oil. Bake 15 minutes, remove from oven and stir. Return to oven for 15 minutes and stir again. Bake 10 minutes (more or less) until carrots and onions are browned and tender when pierced with a knife. (Total roasting time is 40 minutes.) Remove from pan and drizzle with vinegar, stir.

Nutrition facts per serving: 137 calories; 2.3 g protein; 9.0 g fat; 11.0 g carbohydrates; 3.2 g fiber; 220 mg sodium. 6 servings.

Adapted from the Winston-Salem Journal.
Catherine Dancy, Central and Southside Libraries customer. "I love the Library because it's easy to find books online!"

Garlic Rosemary Potatoes

2 lbs. small red potatoes
2 to 3 garlic cloves, minced
1 Tbsp. chopped fresh rosemary or 1½ tsp.
dried rosemary, crushed
3 Tbsp. butter or margarine

Boil potatoes until tender, approximately 20 minutes and drain. While potatoes are cooking, mix remaining ingredients in small microwavable dish. Microwave on medium power until butter melts. Add to potatoes and stir. Note: I like to cut into potatoes a little so they absorb more of butter mixture.

Nutrition facts per serving: 148 calories; 2.7 g protein; 6.1 g fat; 22.1 g carbohydrates; 2.8 g fiber; 66 mg sodium. 6 servings.

Carolyn Price, current staff

Gratin of Root Vegetables

1½ c. heavy cream
2 tsp. salt
2 tsp. ground white pepper
¼ tsp. ground nutmeg
1 large baking potato, peeled and sliced 1/8"
1 large parsnip, peeled and sliced 1/8" *
1 large sweet potato, peeled and sliced 1/8"
1 large turnip, peeled and sliced 1/8" *
½ c. fresh chives, snipped
½ c. freshly grated Parmesan cheese

* may substitute carrots if you prefer

Preheat oven to 350°F. Butter 8"x8"x2" baking dish and set aside. In small bowl, whisk together cream, salt, pepper and nutmeg. Layer half of baking potato slices in prepared baking dish, overlapping them slightly. Drizzle enough of cream mixture over potato to just cover. Layer parsnip slices over potato, then top with sweet potato. Sprinkle the chives and half of Parmesan cheese over sweet potato. Layer turnip slices, then top with remaining baking potato. Pour remaining cream mixture evenly over potato and top with remaining Parmesan. Cover pan with foil.

Bake on lowest rack of oven for 30 minutes. (Put sheet pan underneath to catch any drips.) Remove foil and continue baking for about 30 minutes more, until bubbly and browned on top. Cool on rack for about 10 minutes, then serve warm. Note: Can be prepared several hours ahead; reheat in 300°F oven.

Nutrition facts per serving: 274 calories; 5.0 g protein; 18.5 g fat; 24.4 g carbohydrates; 4.1 g fiber; 729 mg sodium. 8 servings.

Julie James, former staff

Spicy Cauliflower and Potatoes

canola oil for shallow frying
1 lb. boiling potatoes, peeled and cut in thick fries (2"x1"x1")
1 head cauliflower, cut into florets with short stems
¾ tsp. ground ginger
¼ tsp. ground turmeric
1 tsp. ground cumin
1 tsp. ground coriander
1 tsp. salt
¼ tsp. ground cayenne pepper

Put oil in large frying pan and set over medium heat. When oil is hot, put in potatoes and fry until they are golden and almost tender, about 10 minutes. Lift out potatoes and set aside. Turn heat to medium-high, add cauliflower florets to pan and fry for 3 to 4 minutes until they are golden brown. Return potatoes to pan and add all other ingredients. Stir gently to coat vegetables with spices. Add three tablespoons water. Stir once and cover pan. Turn heat down to low and cook very gently for 4 minutes. Serve hot.

Nutrition facts per serving: 177 calories; 4.4 g protein; 9.3 g fat; 21.4 g carbohydrates; 5.6 g fiber; 434 mg sodium. 6 servings.

Andrea Morgan, wife of current staff member Ben Morgan

"Cauliflower is nothing but a cabbage with a college education."

Mark Twain, 1835-1910
Pudd 'n 'head Wilson

Mushroom Rice

1 c. uncooked white rice
1 c. beef broth
2 4-oz. cans mushrooms, not drained
¼ tsp. salt
½ tsp. garlic, minced
⅛ tsp. ground pepper
1 stick (½ c.) butter, melted
1 green pepper, chopped
1 onion, chopped

Preheat oven to 350°F. Mix all ingredients and bake in 1½-quart casserole for 1 hour.

Nutrition facts per serving: 316 calories; 5.9 g protein; 11.8 g fat; 46.5 g carbohydrates; 3.3 g fiber; 686 mg sodium. 4 servings.

Judy Prater, current staff

Ranch Style Baked Beans

1 lb. lean ground beef
3 16-oz. cans pork and beans
1 pkg. dry onion soup mix
2 Tbsp. prepared mustard
2 Tbsp. vinegar
⅔ c. catsup
½ c. water
½ c. chili sauce
dash Worcestershire sauce
dash Tabasco® sauce

Preheat oven to 350°F. Brown ground beef in large pot and drain excess fat. Add remaining ingredients and heat to boil. Pour into large casserole dish and bake for 30 to 45 minutes.

Nutrition facts per serving: 234 calories; 13.5 g protein; 7.7 g fat; 29.7 g carbohydrates; 7.3 g fiber; 1090 mg sodium. 12 servings.

Bob May, former staff

Athens Greek Couscous

2 c. water
1 c. dry couscous
2 cloves garlic, minced
2 Tbsp. olive oil
2 Tbsp. red wine vinegar
½ tsp. salt
½ tsp. ground black pepper
½ tsp. red pepper flakes
½ c. feta cheese, crumbled
½ c. oil-packed sundried tomatoes, drained and chopped
½ c. roasted red peppers, chopped
½ c. fresh chopped basil

Bring water to boil, add couscous, turn off heat and allow to steam for 5 minutes. Fluff with fork. Meanwhile, sauté garlic in olive oil. Mix with vinegar, salt and black and red pepper. Stir feta, tomatoes, roasted peppers and basil into couscous. Drizzle with dressing and toss.

Nutrition facts per serving: 213 calories; 6.2 g protein; 9.4 g fat; 26.6 g carbohydrates; 2.5 g fiber; 395 mg sodium. 6 servings.

Julie Walker, former staff and current PINES Program Director, Georgia Public Library Service

Garlic Cheese Grits

1 c. quick-cooking grits
½ tsp. salt
3 c. water
1 stick (½ c.) margarine
6-oz. roll Kraft® Garlic Cheese
2 eggs
1½ c. milk (approximate)

Preheat oven to 350°F. Cook grits, salt and water in saucepan until thickened. Melt margarine with cheese in separate pan over low heat. Add grits and mix well. Beat eggs in measuring cup. Add enough milk to measure 2 cups. Add to grits and mix well. Spoon into greased 1½-quart baking dish. Bake for 40 minutes.

Nutrition facts per serving: 388 calories; 12.5 g protein; 26.2 g fat; 26.0 g carbohydrates; 0.4 g fiber; 760 mg sodium. 6 servings.

Lara Luck, current staff

Tabouleh

1 c. cracked wheat or bulgur
2 c. boiling water
1 beef or vegetable bouillon cube
¼ c. lemon juice
salt to taste
¼ c. olive oil
1 scallion, minced
1 tomato, diced
½ c. fresh parsley
¼ c. fresh mint (or less if using dried)

Pour boiling water over cracked wheat and bouillon and let stand for half hour, then drain. Mix lemon juice, salt and olive oil and add to cracked wheat. Add rest of ingredients and refrigerate at least an hour before serving. Good as a side dish or an appetizer on baguette slices.

Nutrition facts per serving: 258 calories; 5.1 g protein; 14.1 g fat; 30.4 g carbohydrates; 7.8 g fiber; 375 mg sodium. 4 servings.

Laura Weigand, current staff

Baked Fruit Compote

16-oz. can apricot halves, drained
16-oz. can peach halves, drained
10-oz. pkg. dried plums (prunes)
3 to 4 thin slices of orange
½ c. orange juice
2 Tbsp. butter or margarine, melted
¼ c. firmly packed light brown sugar
½ tsp. grated lemon rind
½ c. coconut (optional)

Preheat oven to 425°F. Put fruit in glass baking dish. Combine juice, butter, sugar and lemon rind in saucepan and heat until sugar melts. Pour over fruit and sprinkle with coconut (if desired). Bake 15 to 20 minutes. Serve warm.

Nutrition Facts: 353 calories; 2.8 g protein; 6.8 g fat; 76.4 g carbohydrates; 7.7 g fiber; 72 mg sodium. 6 servings.

This is great for breakfast, too.
Mitzi Loflin Sapp, Friend of Clemmons Library

"There is no love sincerer than the love of food."

George Bernard Shaw, 1856-1950
Man and Superman

Pineapple Casserole

3 eggs
20-oz. can crushed juice-pack pineapple,
  slightly drained
1 Tbsp. all-purpose flour
½ c. granulated sugar
3 slices white bread, torn into crumbs
1 stick (½ c.) butter, melted

Preheat oven to 400°F. In medium bowl, beat eggs well. Add pineapple, flour and sugar and mix well. Pour into casserole dish. Cover top with bread crumbs. Drizzle with melted butter. Bake for 30 minutes and serve immediately. Note: This is great as a side dish but it can also be served as a dessert with a scoop of vanilla ice cream.

Nutrition facts per serving: 333 calories; 4.3 g protein; 18.3 g fat; 38.0 g carbohydrates; 0.5 g fiber; 273 mg sodium. 6 servings.

My sister, Beth Norwood Stainback, frequently makes this dish for family get-togethers.
Rob Norwood, current staff

Cranberry Relish

1 pkg. strawberry flavor gelatin
1 c. granulated sugar
1 c. boiling water
½ c. lemon juice
¼ c. cold water
1 lb. fresh cranberries
1 med. seedless orange, unpeeled, washed
1 tart apple, unpeeled, washed, cored
  and finely chopped
1 c. pecans, chopped
8-oz. can crushed juice-pack pineapple, drained

Dissolve gelatin and sugar in boiling water. Add lemon juice and cold water. Grind cranberries and orange in meat grinder or food processor. Add to gelatin along with chopped apple, pecans and pineapple. Chill at least 2 hours (preferably more) and serve.

Nutrition facts per serving: 200 calories; 1.6 g protein; 6.6 g fat; 36.0 g carbohydrates; 3.2 g fiber; 24 mg sodium. 12 servings.

Elizabeth Skinner, current staff

BREADS

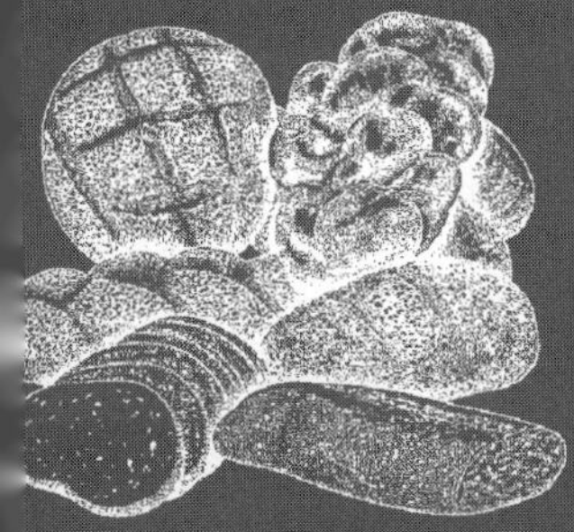
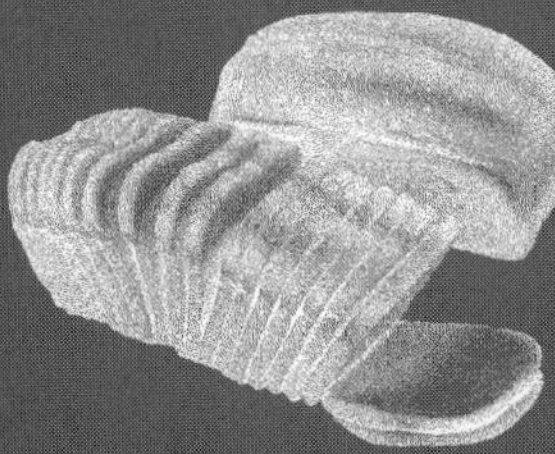
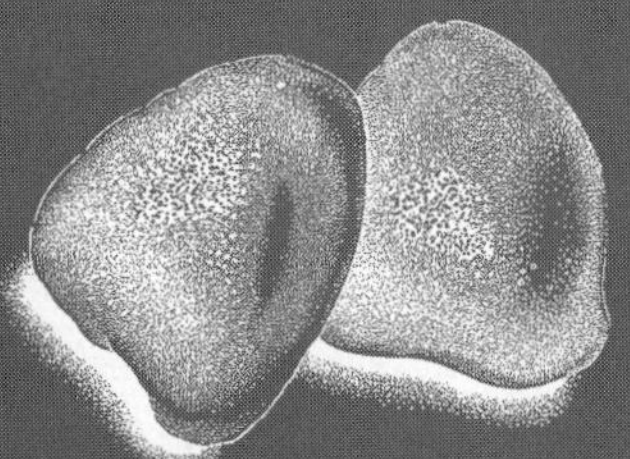

Broccoli Corn Bread

1 stick (½ c.) butter or margarine
1 med. onion, chopped
1 pkg. frozen chopped broccoli
4 eggs, beaten
1 c. cottage cheese
1 tsp. salt
1 pkg. Jiffy® corn muffin mix
½ c. grated cheddar cheese (optional)

Preheat oven to 400°F. Melt butter or margarine in heavy saucepan and add onion. Cook for 7 to 8 minutes, then add broccoli. Cook until broccoli thaws. Remove from heat. Beat eggs, cottage cheese and salt together. Add muffin mix and cooked vegetables to cottage cheese mixture. Mix well. Pour batter into greased 9"x9" baking pan or large cast iron skillet. Top with cheddar cheese, if desired, and bake until firm and lightly browned, about 25 to 35 minutes.

Nutrition facts per serving: 333 calories; 11.2 g protein; 21.1 g fat; 6.5 g carbohydrates; 2.0 g fiber; 879 mg sodium. 8 servings.

Editor's note: Three almost identical recipes were submitted for Broccoli Corn Bread. We'd like to give credit to all three lovely ladies!

I've used this recipe for a very long time. It was given to me by a friend. Her child wouldn't eat vegetables but loved this as the entire meal. A glass of milk sets it off nicely.
Gladys R. Dunnagan, former staff at Reynolda Manor Library

This recipe is from a neighbor.
Hazel Myers, former staff and Friend of the Library. "Books have always been a passion."

Another of my mom's recipes.
Jacquelyn Smith, current staff

"Man is a creature who lives not upon bread alone, but principally by catchwords."

Robert Louis Stevenson, 1850-1894
Virginibus Puerisque and Other Papers

Southern Corn Bread

2 eggs
2 c. buttermilk
2 c. cornmeal
¾ tsp. salt
1 tsp. baking soda
2 tsp. baking powder
2 Tbsp. bacon drippings, melted
(you can substitute shortening or oil)

Preheat oven to 475°F. If you're going to bake in skillet (recommended if you want crispy brown exterior), grease and place pan in oven when it is turned on. It should be smoking hot.

Beat eggs in medium mixing bowl and add buttermilk. Combine dry ingredients and stir into egg mixture. Stir in melted drippings. Pour into hot greased 9" or 10" cast-iron skillet or muffin cups. Bake for 20 to 25 minutes if using skillet or for 15 to 20 minutes for muffins. Variations: Add 3 minced canned or fresh jalapeño peppers, seeds and veins removed. Or add 1 cup creamed corn.

Nutrition facts per serving: 133 calories; 4.3 g protein; 3.5 g fat; 20.2 g carbohydrates; 1.7 g fiber; 389 mg sodium. 12 servings.

Mary McAfee, current staff

Virginia Spoon Bread

½ c. white corn meal
½ c. boiling water
2 Tbsp. bacon drippings, divided
1 tsp. baking powder
½ tsp. salt
1 tsp. granulated sugar
milk (approx. ¼ cup)
2 eggs

Preheat oven to 350°F. Grease small casserole or oven-proof bowl with ½ tablespoon of bacon drippings and place dish in oven to get very hot. In medium bowl, pour boiling water over corn meal and stir to make soft mush. Add remaining ingredients, stirring vigorously, using enough milk to make soupy batter. Very carefully, remove hot baking dish from oven and pour in batter. Return to oven and bake for 30 to 40 minutes or until set but not dry. Serve immediately. Note: If you don't heat the dish and drippings to very hot first, you'll miss the best part—the crispy golden edges!

Nutrition facts per serving: 105 calories; 3.3 g protein; 5.2 g fat; 10.5 g carbohydrates; 0.8 g fiber; 306 mg sodium. 6 servings.

From my mother, a woman who mistakenly thinks she's not much of a cook. She credits this recipe to Nonny, her mother-in-law.
Lise Keppler, current staff

"A land wherein thou shalt eat bread without scarceness."

Holy Bible, Deuteronomy 8:9

Advent Bread

5½ to 6½ c. unsifted all-purpose flour
¾ c. granulated sugar
½ tsp. salt
1 tsp. ground cardamom
2 Tbsp. grated lemon rind (optional)
2 pkgs. active dry yeast
¾ c. milk
½ c. water
1 stick (½ c.) butter
2 eggs, at room temperature
½ c. currants or golden raisins

Plain sugar icing (optional)

½ c. confectioner's sugar
¼ tsp. vanilla extract
2 tsp. warm water (approx.)

In large bowl, thoroughly mix 1½ cup flour, sugar, salt, cardamom, lemon rind and undissolved yeast. In saucepan over low heat, combine milk, water and butter. Heat until warm. Butter does not need to melt. Gradually add to flour mixture and beat until well mixed. Add eggs and 1 cup flour. Beat until blended. Stir in enough additional flour to make soft dough. Turn out onto lightly floured board and knead until smooth and elastic, about 8 to 10 minutes. Place in greased bowl, turning to grease top. Cover and let rise in warm place free from drafts until doubled in bulk, about 1 hour.

Punch dough down and turn out onto lightly floured board. Kneed in currants or raisins. Divide dough into 4 equal pieces, cover and let rest 10 minutes. Shape 3 pieces into smooth balls and flatten slightly. Place balls on greased baking sheet about ½" apart so they look like 3-leaf clover. Cut remaining dough into 4 equal pieces. Roll each piece into 15" rope. Twist ropes together in pairs and press ends to seal. Arrange twisted pairs in cross on cloverleaf. Cover and let rise until doubled in bulk, about 50 minutes. Preheat oven to 350°F. Bake bread for 25 to 30 minutes. If necessary, cover loosely with foil to prevent excess browning. If desired, make icing after bread has cooled by sifting confectioner's sugar into small bowl and stirring in vanilla extract and water, in small increments, until it reaches smooth drizzling consistency. Use icing immediately as it hardens quickly. (Editor's note: This recipe can also be used for Hot Cross Buns at Easter.)

Nutrition facts per serving: 290 calories; 6.6 g protein; 7.1 g fat; 49.6 g carbohydrates; 1.8 g fiber; 147 mg sodium. 16 servings.

Jane Hill, former staff

Cool Rise Bread

2 pkgs. active dry yeast
5½ to 6 c. all-purpose flour
2 Tbsp. granulated sugar
1 Tbsp. salt
1¾ c. milk
½ c. water
3 Tbsp. butter
2 Tbsp. vegetable oil

Thoroughly mix yeast with 2 cups flour, sugar and salt. Heat milk, water and butter over low heat until just warm (105°-110°F). Add milk mixture to flour mixture. Beat for 2 minutes with electric mixer at medium speed. Add 2 more cups of flour and beat on high speed for 2 minutes. Add remaining flour and mix well. Turn out onto lightly floured board. Knead until smooth and springy. Divide into two loaves by rolling out each half of dough to make 8″x12″ rectangle. Break down gas bubbles. Beginning with upper 8″ side, roll toward you like jelly roll. Seal ends and fold sealed ends under. Do not tear dough. Place shaped loaves seam side down in greased loaf pans. Brush with oil and cover with waxed paper. Refrigerate for 2 to 24 hours. Remove from refrigerator and let sit uncovered for 10 minutes. Preheat oven to 400°F. Puncture any gas bubbles and bake loaves 30 to 40 minutes. Remove from pans immediately and brush with butter, if desired.

Nutrition facts per serving: 230 calories; 6.1 g protein; 5.3 g fat; 38.7 g carbohydrates; 1.3 g fiber; 37 mg sodium. 16 servings.

Bill Sugg, former staff

Granny Rolls

1¼ c. water
1 c. whole milk
1 c. granulated sugar
1 pkg. active dry yeast
2 Tbsp. melted vegetable shortening
3 eggs, slightly beaten
6½ c. all-purpose flour, sifted
1½ Tbsp. salt
additional melted shortening for greasing bowl and formed rolls

Combine water and milk in saucepan and heat until lukewarm. Stir in sugar. Add yeast and let sit 5 minutes. Put mixture in large bowl and add melted shortening, eggs and 3 cups flour. Make sure shortening has cooled enough that it won't kill yeast. Mix well. Sift remaining flour and salt together and add to mixture. Knead lightly. Dough should be soft but resilient. If it sticks to your hands, you may need to add more flour. Place in greased bowl, turning once, cover with towel, and let rise until double, 1 to 1½ hours. Punch down. Form rolls in floured hands and place in greased pans. Grease tops of rolls. Cover lightly and let rise until double (1 hour). Preheat oven to 350ºF. Bake rolls for 20 to 30 minutes or until golden brown. Notes: Whole milk can be replaced with evaporated milk for slightly richer rolls. For best results, use straight-sided dark aluminum pans. Makes excellent sweet rolls, too!

Nutrition facts per serving: 127 calories; 3.2 g protein; 2.2 g fat; 23.2 g carbohydrates; 0.6 g fiber; 300 mg sodium. 36 rolls.

When I was little, I thought all grandmothers smelled like yeast. Mine certainly did. Enjoy these rolls with dinner or put a thick slice of homegrown tomato and a bit of Virginia ham in the middle for an exceptional lunch.
Lise Keppler, current staff

Ice Box Rolls

1 c. boiling water
1 c. shortening
½ c. granulated sugar
1½ tsp. salt
2 eggs, beaten
2 pkgs. active dry yeast
1 c. lukewarm water
6 c. unsifted all-purpose flour

Pour boiling water over shortening, sugar and salt. Blend and let cool. Add beaten eggs. Let yeast stand in lukewarm water for 5 minutes. Stir yeast, then combine both mixtures. Add flour and blend. Knead, adding as little flour as possible. Roll out and make into desired shapes in greased pans. Let rise for 1½ hours. Preheat oven to 450ºF, then bake rolls for 15 to 20 minutes or until lightly browned.

Nutrition facts per serving: 107 calories; 2.0 g protein; 4.6 g fat; 14.1 g carbohydrates; 0.4 g fiber; 76 mg sodium. 48 rolls.

When I was teaching in Guilford County (1964), a cohort shared this recipe, which had been in her family for 100 years. Donna L. Staley, Chairman of the Forsyth County Library Board of Trustees. "The library is a welcoming place. The staff is friendly, helpful, and prompt in meeting requests for information."

Tender Dinner Knots

1 pkg. active dry yeast
¼ c. warm water (110° to 115°)
1 c. warm milk (110° to 115°)
1 egg
2 Tbsp. granulated sugar
2 Tbsp. shortening, melted
1 tsp. salt
3½ to 4 c. all-purpose flour

In large mixing bowl, dissolve yeast in warm water. Add milk, egg, sugar, shortening, salt and 2 cups flour. Beat until smooth. Stir in enough remaining flour to form soft dough. Turn onto floured surface and knead until smooth and elastic, about 6 to 8 minutes. Place in greased bowl, turning once to grease top. Cover and let rise in warm place until doubled, about 1 hour. Punch down dough. Turn onto lightly floured surface, shape into 32 pieces and place in greased pans. (You can form "knots" by rolling dough pieces into thick rope and tying single knot.) Cover and let rise in warm place again until doubled. Preheat oven to 425°F and bake for 10 to 15 minutes or until golden brown.

Nutrition facts per serving: 75 calories; 2.2 g protein; 1.4 g fat; 13.1 g carbohydrates; 0.4 g fiber; 6 mg sodium. 32 rolls.

Juanita A. Tatum, Forsyth County Public Library Board of Trustees

Quick and Easy Herb Bread

¼ c. olive oil
4 to 6 Tbsp. minced fresh herbs (dill, basil, fennel, or oregano alone or in combination)
10 frozen biscuits

Preheat oven to 350°F. Pour olive oil in large loaf pan. Sprinkle herbs on oil. Add biscuits to herb oil, thoroughly coating each piece. Bake 40 to 45 minutes. Bread pulls apart when it is served. Leftovers (if there are any) may be frozen.

Nutrition facts per serving: 259 calories; 5.1 g protein; 14.4 g fat; 26.1 g carbohydrates; 1.1 g fiber; 531 mg sodium. 10 servings.

Served at Cooking With Herbs program, part of "Successful Gardening at the Library" series.
Yolanda Pickett, Extension Agent, NC Cooperative Extension Service

"Music I heard with you was more than music,
And bread I broke with you was more than bread."

Conrad Aiken, 1889-1973
Bread and Music

Mom's Whole Wheat Bread

2 pkgs. active dry yeast
2¼ c. warm water, divided
⅓ c. honey
1 Tbsp. salt
¼ c. shortening, melted and cooled
6 to 7 c. whole wheat flour
soft margarine or butter

Dissolve yeast in ½ cup warm water and let sit for 5 minutes to activate yeast. Stir in honey, salt, shortening, 1¾ cups water and 3½ cups flour. Beat until smooth. Mix in enough remaining flour to make dough easy to handle. Turn dough onto lightly floured surface. Knead about 10 minutes or until smooth and elastic. Place in greased bowl and turn greased side up. Cover and let rise in warm place until doubled, about 1 hour.

Grease 2 loaf pans. Punch down dough and divide in half. Roll each half into rectangle about 9"x18". Roll up, beginning at short side. With side of hand, press each end to seal. Fold ends under loaf. Place each loaf, seam side down in pan. Cover and let rise until doubled, about 1 hour.

Preheat oven to 375ºF. Place loaves on low rack so that tops of pans are in center of oven. Pans should not touch oven sides or each other. Bake 40 to 45 minutes or until deep golden brown and loaves sound hollow when tapped. Remove from pans. Brush loaves with soft margarine or butter. Cool on wire racks.

Nutrition facts per serving: 115 calories; 3.7 g protein; 2.0 g fat; 22.2 g carbohydrates; 3.4 g fiber; 220 mg sodium. 32 servings (2 loaves).

This is my mom's recipe.
Mary McAfee, current staff

"Poetry is an act of peace. Peace goes into the making of a poet as flour goes into the making of bread."

Pablo Neruda, 1904-1973
Confieso Que He Vivido: Memorias

CAKES

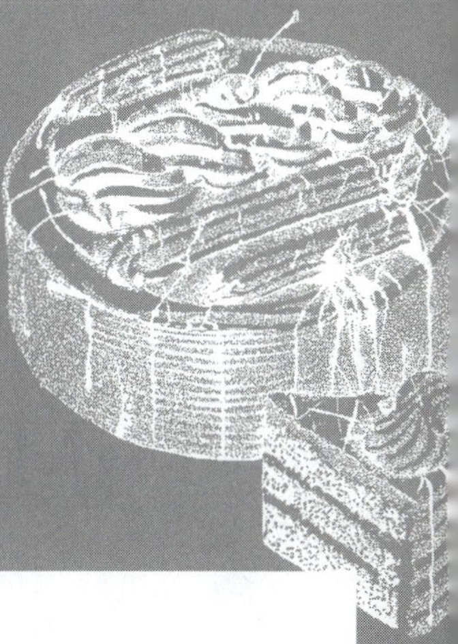

Apple Pound Cake

- 3 c. all-purpose flour
- 1 tsp. baking soda
- 1 tsp. salt
- ½ tsp. ground cinnamon
- ½ tsp. ground nutmeg
- 1½ c. corn oil
- 2 c. granulated sugar
- 3 eggs
- 2 tsp. vanilla extract
- 2 c. apple, chopped
- 1 c. pecans, chopped
- ½ c. raisins

Preheat oven to 325ºF. Combine flour, baking soda, salt, cinnamon and nutmeg. In large bowl, beat oil, sugar, eggs and vanilla together at medium speed. Gradually beat in flour mixture until smooth. Fold in apples, pecans and raisins. Turn into greased and floured tube pan. Bake for 1 hour or until cake tests done. Cool in pan for 10 minutes.

Nutrition facts per serving: 448 calories; 4.3 g protein; 26.5 g fat; 50.1 g carbohydrates; 1.8 g fiber; 237 mg sodium. 16 servings.

Hazel Myers, former staff and Friend of Clemmons Library

Big Mama's Apple Cake

- 1¼ c. vegetable oil
- 2 c. granulated sugar
- 3 eggs
- 2½ c. all-purpose flour
- 1 tsp. salt
- 1 tsp. baking soda
- 2 tsp. baking powder
- 1 tsp. ground cinnamon
- 1 tsp. ground allspice
- 1 tsp. vanilla extract
- 3 c. tart apples, cored, peeled and chopped fine
- 1 c. walnuts or pecans, chopped

Preheat oven to 350ºF. Combine oil, sugar and eggs in bowl and beat well. Sift flour, salt, baking soda, baking powder and spices together. Add sifted ingredients to sugar mixture and beat well. Add vanilla and beat. Fold in apples and nuts and pour into greased and floured tube pan. Bake for 1 hour or until toothpick comes out clean.

Nutrition facts per serving: 406 calories; 4.3 g protein; 23.0 g fat; 47.4 g carbohydrates; 2.2 g fiber; 298 mg sodium. 16 servings.

This family recipe came from my grandmother, who we called Big Mama. She lived on a farm outside Yazoo City, Mississippi. I remember she lived in an old house without running water. Whenever you needed water, you took a bucket out to the cistern, a large container for rainwater located near the house. She had an entire orchard full of tart apples.
Merrikay Brown, current staff

Fresh Apple Cake

1 c. Crisco® shortening
2 c. granulated sugar
3 eggs
2 c. all-purpose flour
1 tsp. baking soda
½ tsp. ground nutmeg
½ tsp. ground cinnamon
3 c. diced apples

Topping

½ stick (4 Tbsp.) margarine
½ c. milk
1 c. packed brown sugar

Preheat oven to 325°F. Cream shortening, add sugar and mix well. Add eggs one at a time, beating after each addition. Combine dry ingredients and add slowly. Stir in apples. Spray 9"x13" baking pan with cooking spray. Spread batter in pan and bake 45 to 50 minutes. (Time depends on how moist, firm, or soft apples are.) When cake is done, top will crack or fall when stuck with knife in center. While cake is still hot, prepare topping by boiling margarine, milk and brown sugar together for 3 minutes. Poke holes in cake with fork and pour topping over it.

Nutrition facts per serving: 503 calories; 4.0 g protein; 22.7 g fat; 72.6 g carbohydrates; 1.3 g fiber; 178 mg sodium. 12 servings.

This was my mother Sue Dell Hall's recipe. It's a great fall/winter dessert after a meal of homemade soup.
Vicki H. Davis, Friend of the Library

Best Coconut Cake

1 box white cake mix
eggs, oil and water as required by cake mix
12 oz. Cool Whip® whipped topping, thawed
8-oz. can cream of coconut (look in mixed drinks area at grocery store)
2 8-oz. pkgs. frozen unsweetened coconut

Prepare cake in 9"x13" pan according to package directions. When cake has baked and is still hot, poke holes all over. Pour cream of coconut over cake and let it cool. Sprinkle one package of coconut over cooled cake. Frost cake with Cool Whip®, then sprinkle with remaining package of coconut. Refrigerate.

Nutrition facts per serving: 449 calories; 4.3 g protein; 27.8 g fat; 47.2 g carbohydrates; 5.1 g fiber; 314 mg sodium. 12 servings.

This cake is so easy to make and very moist.
Elaine Childress, Friend of Southside Branch Library

Orange Coconut Cake

2/3 stick (1/3 c.) butter
1/3 c. vegetable shortening
1½ c. granulated sugar
2 tsp. grated orange rind
3 eggs
2½ c. sifted cake flour (or all-purpose flour sifted with 5 Tbsp. cornstarch)
2½ tsp. baking powder
1 tsp. salt
1 c. orange juice
3½-oz. can flaked coconut
1 orange, sectioned

Filling

2/3 c. granulated sugar
2 Tbsp. all-purpose flour
1 c. orange juice
2 egg yolks
2 Tbsp. butter or margarine

1 recipe Seven-Minute Frosting (see page 81)

Preheat oven to 350ºF. Cream together butter, shortening, sugar and orange rind. Add eggs one at a time, beating well after each addition. Combine cake flour, baking powder and salt. Add to creamed mixture alternately with orange juice, beginning and ending with flour. Turn batter into 2 greased and lined 9" round cake pans. Bake about 25 minutes. While cake is cooling, prepare filling.

To prepare filling, mix sugar and flour in saucepan. Add orange juice and egg yolks. Place over medium heat and bring to a boil, stirring constantly. Cook one minute. Add butter and stir well. Cool before using.

To construct dessert, place one layer of cooled cake on plate. Spread orange filling to edge. Place second layer on top. Frost top and sides with Seven-Minute Frosting. Sprinkle top and sides with coconut. Place orange sections pinwheel fashion in center of cake.

Nutrition facts per serving(frosted): 572 calories; 5.9 g protein; 18.7 g fat; 97.2 g carbohydrates; 1.4 g fiber; 423 mg sodium. 12 servings.

This was my father's, Mike Dale Everett, favorite cake. My mother always made it for him on his birthday, March 30. He died at age 70 in 1998. Every year, when I can, I make that cake around his birthday and think of him when I eat it.
Merrikay Brown, current staff

"And eat thy fill! It's Heaven's sugar cake."

Edward Taylor, 1644-1729
Sacramental Meditations

Seven-Minute Frosting

2 egg whites
1 Tbsp. light corn syrup
5 Tbsp. water
1½ c. granulated sugar
¼ tsp. cream of tartar
1 tsp. vanilla extract

Combine all ingredients except vanilla in top of double boiler. Beat 1 minute on high speed to blend. Place over boiling water and beat until mixture forms peaks when beater is raised, about 7 minutes. Remove from boiling water, add vanilla and continue beating until thick enough to spread.

Nutrition facts per serving: 106 calories; 0.7 g protein; 0 g fat; 26.4 g carbohydrates; 0 g fiber; 11 mg sodium. 12 servings.

Merrikay Brown, current staff

Big Mama's Lemon Pound Cake

1 stick (½ c.) butter, softened
½ c. shortening
2 c. granulated sugar
4 eggs, separated
3 c. all-purpose flour
1 tsp. baking powder
1 c. milk
1 Tbsp. vanilla extract
1 Tbsp. lemon extract
1 recipe Lemon Frosting (see page 82)

Preheat oven to 325°F. Cream butter, shortening and sugar together. Add one egg yolk at a time to creamed mixture, beating well after each addition. Sift flour and baking powder together in separate bowl. Alternately add flour mixture and milk to creamed mixture. In separate bowl, beat egg whites. Fold into batter. Stir in vanilla and lemon extracts. Grease and line bottom of tube pan with two layers of brown paper. Pour mixture into pan. Bake for 60 minutes. Cool and ice with lemon frosting.

Nutrition facts per serving (unfrosted): 319 calories; 4.5 g protein; 14.1 g fat; 43.9 g carbohydrates; 0.6 g fiber; 113 mg sodium. 12 servings.

This recipe is a family favorite. My mother, the late Thelma Norwood Holtzclaw, always made this pound cake for birthdays, holidays and other special occasions. After her death, her favorite recipes, including this one, were given to me.
Sylvia Sprinkle-Hamlin, Director, Forsyth County Public Library

Lemon Frosting

- 1 stick (½ c.) butter, softened
- 1 lb. confectioner's sugar
- juice of 2 fresh lemons

Cream butter in medium bowl. Add ⅓ of confectioner's sugar and beat well. Add 2 teaspoons lemon juice and beat again. Repeat alternate addition of sugar and lemon juice, beating until smooth after each addition. Only use as much lemon juice as you need to reach good spreading consistency.

Nutrition facts per serving: 178 calories; 0.1 g protein; 7.7 g fat; 28.3 g carbohydrates; 0 g fiber; 78 mg sodium. 12 servings.

Sylvia Sprinkle-Hamlin, Director, Forsyth County Public Library

Cherry Pound Cake

- 1 c. shortening
- ½ c. margarine
- 3 c. granulated sugar
- 6 eggs
- ½ tsp. vanilla extract
- ½ tsp. almond extract
- ¾ c. milk
- 3¾ c. all-purpose flour
- ½ 10-oz. bottle maraschino cherries, drained and chopped
- 1 recipe Cherry Frosting (see page 83)

Cream shortening and margarine. Add sugar gradually. Add eggs one at a time, beating well after each addition. Add vanilla and almond extracts to milk. Add flour and flavored milk alternately to creamed mixture, beating well after each addition. Fold in cherries. Pour batter into greased and floured loaf pan. Place cake in cold oven, turn heat to 350ºF and bake for 40 to 45 minutes or until toothpick inserted in center comes out clean. Let cake cool completely before frosting.

Nutrition facts per serving (unfrosted): 656 calories; 7.7 g protein; 31.7 g fat; 86.2 g carbohydrates; 1.4 g fiber; 180 mg sodium. 12 servings.

Jane Jester, former staff

"Would ye both eat your cake and have your cake?"

John Haywood, 1497-1580
Proverbs

Cherry Frosting

½ stick (4 Tbsp.) margarine, softened
3 oz. cream cheese, softened
1 tsp. vanilla or almond extract
2 c. confectioner's sugar
½ c. finely chopped nuts
½ 10-oz. bottle maraschino cherries, drained and chopped
½ c. flaked coconut

Cream margarine and cream cheese together. Add vanilla or almond extract. Gradually add confectioner's sugar, beating well after each addition. Fold in nuts, cherries and coconut. Frost cooled cake.

Nutrition facts per serving: 208 calories; 1.1 g protein; 5.0 g fat; 27.6 g carbohydrates; 1.0 g fiber; 71 mg sodium. 12 servings.

Jane Jester, former staff

7-Up® Pound Cake

2 sticks (1 c.) butter
½ c. shortening
3 c. granulated sugar
5 eggs
3 c. cake flour
12-oz. can 7-Up® lemon-lime soda
1 tsp. vanilla extract
1 tsp. lemon extract

Preheat oven to 300°F. Cream butter, shortening and sugar together until fluffy. Add eggs one at a time, beating slowly. Add flour, 7-Up® and extracts and beat well. Pour batter into greased and floured 10" tube pan or Bundt® pan. Bake for 60 minutes, then reduce heat to 250°F and bake for 15 minutes more or until toothpick inserted in cake comes out clean.

Nutrition facts per serving: 431 calories; 4.1 g protein; 19.7 g fat; 60.3 g carbohydrates; 0.4 g fiber; 140 mg sodium. 16 servings.

Annie Johnson, former staff

Chocolate on Chocolate Cake

1 stick (½ c.) butter or margarine
4 Tbsp. unsweetened cocoa powder
1 c. corn oil
1 c. water
2 c. all-purpose flour
2 c. granulated sugar
2 eggs
1 tsp. baking soda
½ c. buttermilk

Icing

1 stick (½ c.) butter
4 Tbsp. unsweetened cocoa powder
3 Tbsp. milk (approximate)
1 Tbsp. vanilla extract
1 lb. (1 box) confectioner's sugar

Preheat oven to 350ºF. Heat butter, cocoa, oil and water together in saucepan until butter is melted. Mix well. Aerate flour with fork and mix it with sugar in medium or large bowl. Pour heated mixture over flour and sugar. Add eggs and mix together. Dissolve baking soda in buttermilk and add to batter. Pour into 9"x13" pan. Bake for 30 to 35 minutes or until cake tests done. Prepare icing by mixing all ingredients together, adding more milk as necessary to reach spreading consistency. Spread icing on hot cake.

Nutrition facts per serving: 636 calories; 4.5 g protein; 35.4 g fat; 79.0 g carbohydrates; 1.7 g fiber; 286 mg sodium. 12 servings.

This recipe was in the Winston-Salem Journal *in Beth Tartan's column many years ago. It is a very moist cake.*
Valena V. Vogler, past staff (1956-1986) at Main and Adult Outreach

Six-Minute Chocolate Cake

1½ c. unbleached all-purpose flour
1/3 c. unsweetened cocoa powder
1 tsp. baking soda
½ tsp. salt
1 c. granulated sugar
½ c. vegetable oil
1 c. cold water or brewed coffee (I use ½ and ½)
1 tsp. vanilla extract
1 tsp. almond extract
2 Tbsp. distilled vinegar

Glaze

½ lb. bittersweet chocolate
¾ c. water, milk, or half-and-half, hot
½ tsp. vanilla extract

Preheat oven to 375ºF. Sift together flour, cocoa, baking soda, salt and sugar into ungreased 8" square or 9" round baking pan. In 2-cup measuring cup, measure and mix together oil, water or coffee and vanilla and almond extracts. Pour liquid ingredients into baking pan and mix batter with fork or small whisk. When batter is smooth, add vinegar and stir quickly. There will be pale swirls in batter where baking soda and vinegar are reacting. Stir just until vinegar is evenly distributed throughout batter. Bake for 25 to 30 minutes. Set cake aside to cool.

To make glaze, reset oven to 300°F. Melt chocolate in small ovenproof bowl or heavy skillet in oven for about 15 minutes. Stir hot liquid and vanilla into chocolate until smooth. Spoon glaze over cooled cake. Refrigerate glazed cake for at least 30 minutes before serving.

Nutrition facts per serving (glaze made with milk): 314 calories; 3.6 g protein; 15.5 g fat; 42.7 g carbohydrates; 2.3 g fiber; 213 mg sodium. 12 servings.

Andrea Morgan, wife of current staff member Ben Morgan

Toll House® Cake

- 1 stick (½ c.) butter, softened
- 1½ c. firmly packed brown sugar
- 1 tsp. vanilla extract
- 2 eggs
- 2¼ c. unsifted all-purpose flour
- 1½ tsp. baking soda
- 1 tsp. salt
- 1¼ c. milk
- 1 c. (6 oz.) Nestlé Toll House Mini Morsels®
- 1 recipe Rich and Creamy Chocolate Frosting (see below)

Preheat oven to 350°F. In large bowl, combine butter, brown sugar and vanilla, beating until creamy. Add eggs, one at a time, beating well after each addition. Sift together flour, baking soda and salt. Alternately add flour mixture and milk to creamed mixture. Stir in Mini Morsels®. Pour into two 9" cake pans or one 10" Bundt® pan, greased and floured. Bake in 9" pans for 35 minutes or in Bundt® pan for 45 to 50 minutes. Cool 15 minutes before icing with Rich and Creamy Chocolate Frosting.

Nutrition facts per serving (frosted): 587 calories; 5.7 g protein; 23.2 g fat; 93.7 g carbohydrates; 2.2 g fiber; 571 mg sodium. 12 servings.

Vicki Taylor, current staff

Rich and Creamy Chocolate Frosting

- ⅔ stick (⅓ c.) butter
- 1 c. (6 oz.) Nestlé Toll House Mini Morsels®
- ¼ tsp. salt
- 1 tsp. vanilla extract
- 3 c. confectioner's sugar
- 5 Tbsp. milk

Melt butter in small saucepan. Stir in Mini Morsels® until melted. Transfer to small bowl. Add salt and vanilla extract. Alternately add confectioner's sugar and milk in small quantities, beating well until creamy and smooth.

Nutrition facts per serving: 234 calories; 0.8 g protein; 9.5 g fat; 38.9 g carbohydrates; 0.8 g fiber; 106 mg sodium. 12 servings.

Vicki Taylor, current staff

Lane Cake

2 sticks (1 c.) butter or margarine, softened
2 c. granulated sugar
3¼ c. all-purpose flour
1 Tbsp. baking powder
¾ tsp. salt
1 c. milk
1 tsp. vanilla extract
8 egg whites, stiffly beaten

Filling

8 egg yolks
1½ c. granulated sugar
1 stick (½ c.) butter or margarine
1 c. chopped pecans
1 c. flaked coconut
½ c. bourbon
½ c. maraschino cherries, drained
1 c. raisins

½ recipe Seven-Minute Frosting (see page 81)
pecan halves (optional)

Preheat oven to 325ºF. Cream butter, gradually adding sugar and beating well at medium speed. Combine flour, baking powder and salt. Add flour mixture to creamed mixture alternately with milk, beginning and ending with flour mixture. Mix after each addition. Stir in vanilla. Fold in egg whites. Pour batter into 3 greased and floured 9″ round cake pans. Bake 25 minutes or until toothpick inserted in center comes out clean. Cool in pans 10 minutes. Remove from pans and let cool completely on wire racks.

To prepare filling, combine egg yolks, sugar and butter in heavy saucepan. Cook over medium heat, stirring constantly, until thickened, about 20 minutes. Remove from heat and stir in pecans, coconut, bourbon, cherries and raisins. Cool completely.

To assemble cake, spread filling between layers and on top of cake. Spread Seven-Minute Frosting on sides. Garnish with pecan halves, if desired.

Nutrition facts per serving (frosted, without pecan halves): 670 calories; 8.0 g protein; 27.5 g fat; 98.2 g carbohydrates; 2.1 g fiber; 441 mg sodium. 16 servings.

Served at On The Same Page program featuring To Kill a Mockingbird *by Harper Lee.*
Merrikay Brown, current staff

Italian Cream Cake

5 eggs, separated
1 stick (½ c.)butter
½ c. vegetable oil
2 c. granulated sugar
2 c. self-rising flour
1 tsp. baking soda
1 c. buttermilk
1 tsp. vanilla extract
1 c. chopped pecans
1 c. coconut
1 recipe Cream Cheese Frosting (see below)

Preheat oven to 350ºF. Beat egg whites until stiff. In large bowl, cream butter and oil together. Add sugar and beat until smooth. Add egg yolks and beat again. Sift flour and soda together. Add to creamed mixture alternately with buttermilk. Stir in vanilla. Add coconut and nuts. Fold in beaten egg whites. Pour into 2 greased and floured cake pans. Bake for 25 minutes. Allow cake to cool before icing with cream cheese frosting.

Nutrition facts per serving(frosted): 796 calories; 8.6 g protein; 49.3 g fat; 84.5 g carbohydrates; 2.7 g fiber; 650 mg sodium. 12 servings.

Judy Prater, current staff

Cream Cheese Frosting

8 oz. cream cheese, softened
1 stick (½ c.) butter
1 lb. confectioner's sugar
1 tsp. vanilla extract
1 c. chopped nuts

Beat cream cheese and butter until smooth. Add sugar and vanilla and blend well. Fold in nuts.

Nutrition facts per serving: 304 calories; 2.3 g protein; 20.8 g fat; 29.3 g carbohydrates; 0.9 g fiber; 134 mg sodium. 12 servings.

Judy Prater and Elizabeth Skinner, current staff

"At length I recollected the thoughtless saying of a great princess, who, on being informed that the country people had no bread, replied, 'Let them eat cake.'"

Jean Jacques Rousseau, 1712-1778
Confessions, Bk. VI

Sock-It-To-Me Cake

1 box yellow cake mix
1 c. sour cream
½ c. granulated sugar
¾ c. vegetable oil
4 eggs
3 Tbsp. brown sugar
1 tsp. ground cinnamon
½ c. chopped nuts

Glaze

1 c. confectioner's sugar
1 tsp. vanilla extract
3 tsp. milk

Preheat oven to 350ºF. Blend cake mix, sour cream, sugar and oil. Add eggs 1 at a time, beating well after each addition. Pour half of batter into greased and floured Bundt® or pound cake pan. Mix together brown sugar, cinnamon and nuts and sprinkle on batter. Pour rest of batter on top of nut mixture. Bake for 55 minutes. Cool for 10 minutes, then remove from pan. Prepare glaze by mixing together confectioner's sugar, vanilla and milk. Pour on hot cake.

Nutrition facts per serving: 488 calories; 5.0 g protein; 27.7 g fat; 56.3 g carbohydrates; 0.9 g fiber; 320 mg sodium. 12 servings.

Mary Dula, current staff

Strawberry Shortcake

½ c. shortening
1½ c. granulated sugar
4 eggs
2¼ c. all-purpose flour
1 Tbsp. baking powder
¼ tsp. salt
1 c. milk
1 tsp. vanilla extract
6 c. fresh or frozen strawberries
2 c. whipping cream

Preheat oven to 350ºF. In mixing bowl, blend shortening, sugar and eggs together. Sift flour, baking powder and salt together. Alternate gradually adding dry ingredients and milk to sugar mixture. Beat with electric mixer for about 3 minutes, scraping sides and bottom of bowl. Add vanilla and mix well. Pour equal amounts in 4 lightly greased 9" cake pans. Bake for 20 minutes. Remove from oven and let cool. Just before serving, whip cream until stiff. To assemble dessert, put layer of strawberries and whipped cream between each layer of shortcake.

Nutrition facts per serving: 458 calories; 6.4 g protein; 26.2 g fat; 51.6 g carbohydrates; 2.5 g fiber; 218 mg sodium. 12 servings.

Butch Allred, former staff

Three Sisters' Carrot Cake

1½ c. granulated sugar
2 c. all-purpose flour, sifted
2 tsp. baking soda
1 Tbsp. ground cinnamon
1 tsp. salt
1⅓ c. vegetable oil
4 eggs, beaten
3 c. carrots, grated in food processor
(1 lb. of baby carrots)
1 recipe Cream Cheese Frosting (see page 87)

Preheat oven to 350ºF. Mix sugar, flour, baking soda, cinnamon and salt. Add oil, beaten eggs and grated carrots. Mix well. Pour into three 8″ (or two 9″) cake pans and bake 30 to 35 minutes. Allow cake to cool before frosting.

Nutrition facts per serving (frosted): 727 calories; 6.6 g protein; 46.9 g fat; 73.2 g carbohydrates; 2.2 g fiber; 582 mg sodium. 12 servings.

The Three Sisters are my sisters and me. This cake was first baked by my sister, Carole. Now we all bake it for special occasions and my girls request it for their birthday cake.
Elizabeth Skinner, current staff

"An I had but one penny in the world, thou shouldst have it to buy gingerbread."

William Shakespeare, 1564-1616
Love's Labour's Lost, Act V, Scene i

Southern Gingerbread and Lemon Sauce

- 3 eggs
- 1 c. granulated sugar
- 1 c. molasses
- 1 c. shortening
- 1 tsp. ground cinnamon
- 1 tsp. ground ginger (or more for spicier flavor)
- 1 tsp. ground cloves
- 2 tsp. baking soda
- 2 Tbsp. hot water
- 2 c. all-purpose flour
- 1 c. boiling water

Lemon Sauce

- ½ c. granulated sugar
- 4 tsp. cornstarch
- ¼ tsp. salt
- 1 c. water
- 2 Tbsp. butter
- 1½ Tbsp. lemon juice
- 1 tsp. grated lemon rind

Preheat oven to 325ºF. Mix eggs, sugar, molasses, shortening and spices in large bowl and beat well. Dissolve soda in hot water and add to beaten mixture. Sift flour into mixture and beat well. Add boiling water and beat lightly and quickly. Pour into 1 9″x13″ or 2 9″ cake pans. Bake 35 to 45 minutes or until toothpick inserted in center comes out clean.

To make sauce, combine sugar, cornstarch and salt in saucepan. Mix well. Add water and cook over low heat for 5 minutes or until clear and thickened. Remove from heat and stir in butter, lemon juice and lemon rind. Serve hot over warm gingerbread.

Nutrition facts per serving: 458 calories; 6.4 g protein; 26.2 g fat; 51.6 g carbohydrates; 2.5 g fiber; 218 mg sodium. 16 servings.

From Grandmother Wheeless, my husband's grandmother.
Kathleen Wheeless, current staff

Pumpkin Crisp Cake

3 c. (2 cans) cooked pumpkin
12-oz. can evaporated milk
1 c. granulated sugar
½ tsp. ground cinnamon
3 eggs
1 box yellow cake mix
1 c. chopped nuts
2 sticks (1 c.) butter, melted and cooled

Topping

8 oz. cream cheese, softened
8 oz. Cool Whip® whipped topping, thawed
1½ c. confectioner's sugar

Preheat oven to 350°F. Mix pumpkin, milk, sugar, cinnamon and eggs. Pour mixture in 9″x13″ pan lined with waxed paper or parchment. Crumble cake mix over pumpkin mixture. Crumble nuts over cake mix. Drizzle melted butter over top. Bake for 50 to 60 minutes. Remove cake from oven and turn upside down. Remove waxed paper and let cool. Mix all topping ingredients together and spread on top of cake. Refrigerate. Notes: I turn this upside down onto another 9″x13″ pan. May be made ahead and frozen.

Nutrition facts per serving: 347 calories; 3.9 g protein; 19.8 g fat; 39.9 g carbohydrates; 1.7 g fiber; 269 mg sodium. 24 servings.

Brenda Israel, wife of Jim Israel, Board member of Friends of Clemmons Library

Rum Cake

½ c. chopped pecans
1 box yellow cake mix ("pudding" or "moist" type)
4 eggs
½ c. vegetable oil
½ c. dark rum
½ c. water

Glaze

1 stick (½ c.) butter
¼ c. water
1 c. granulated sugar
½ c. dark rum

Preheat oven to 350°F. Grease and flour Bundt® cake pan and sprinkle with nuts. Combine cake mix, eggs, oil, rum and water in large bowl and mix at medium speed until well combined. Pour into prepared pan and bake 45 minutes or until toothpick inserted in center comes out clean. While cake is baking, prepare glaze by melting butter in saucepan with water and sugar. Bring to light boil, remove from heat and add rum. Once cake has been out of oven for 5 minutes, poke holes in top and sides using small sharp knife (such as steak knife). Drizzle glaze all over hot cake and let cool completely before serving.

Nutrition facts per serving: 252 calories; 2.2 g protein; 13.4 g fat; 25.9 g carbohydrates; 0.5 g fiber; 193 mg sodium. 24 servings.

Claudette Weston, co-chair Library and History Museum Foundation
Editor's note: Ms. Weston and her family prepare hundreds—no exaggeration—of these cakes at Christmas time. She delivers one to the library every year!

Cream Cheese Cake

1½ c. graham cracker crumbs
1 stick (½ c.) butter, melted
½ c. finely chopped nuts
½ tsp. ground cinnamon
16 oz. cream cheese, softened
1 c. granulated sugar
3 eggs
½ tsp. salt
2 tsp. vanilla extract
½ tsp. almond extract
3 c. sour cream

Preheat oven to 375ºF. Combine graham cracker crumbs, melted butter, nuts and cinnamon. Pack into spring-form pan on bottom and up sides. Cream together cream cheese and sugar. Add eggs, salt and extracts. Beat until smooth. Blend in sour cream. Pour into crust-lined pan. If crumbs are higher than mixture, run spoon around to make edge. Bake 35 to 45 minutes. Remove from oven when center springs back, even if it seems loose to you. Cool on rack for 30 minutes, then refrigerate 4 to 5 hours.

Nutrition facts per serving: 353 calories; 5.4 g protein; 26.1 g fat; 26.0 g carbohydrates; 0.6 g fiber; 277 mg sodium. 16 servings.

Jean Godfrey Block, current staff

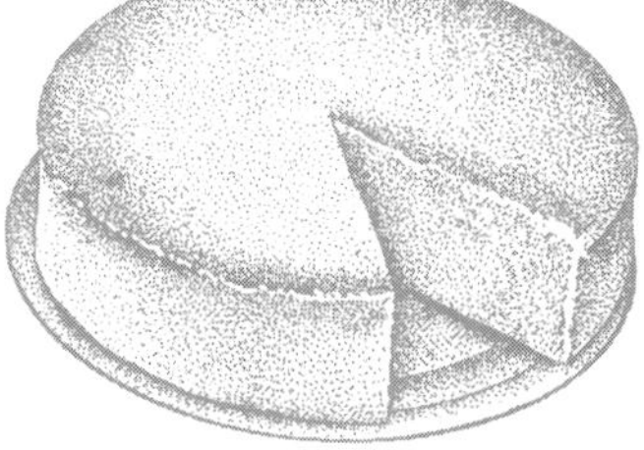

Robert's Ginger Cheesecake

16 oz. cream cheese, softened
½ c. + 2 Tbsp. granulated sugar, divided
2 eggs
2 tsp. lemon juice
1 to 2 Tbsp. freshly grated ginger
1 unbaked pie shell
¾ c. sour cream
1 Tbsp. slivered crystallized ginger

Preheat oven to 350ºF. Blend cream cheese, ½ cup sugar, eggs, lemon juice and grated ginger until smooth. Pour into pie shell. Bake for 20 to 25 minutes. Mix sour cream, remaining sugar and crystallized ginger. Spread over filling while still hot. Turn oven off and return cheesecake to oven for a few minutes. Remove and chill well.

Nutrition facts per serving: 261 calories; 3.6 g protein; 19.8 g fat; 18.5 g carbohydrates; 0.1 g fiber; 188 mg sodium. 12 servings.

Robert Burgin, former staff and current President, North Carolina Library Association

PIES

Apple Pie

4 lg. tart apples
1 unbaked 9" pie shell
1 c. granulated sugar, divided
1 tsp. ground cinnamon
¾ c. all-purpose flour
$^2/_3$ stick ($^1/_3$ c.) butter or margarine

Preheat oven to 400°F. Pare apples, cut in eighths and arrange in pie shell. Mix ½ cup sugar with cinnamon and sprinkle over apples. Sift remaining ½ cup sugar with flour. Cut in butter until crumbly. Sprinkle over apples. Bake 40 to 50 minutes.

Nutrition facts per serving: 345 calories; 2.1 g protein; 12.9 g fat; 56.2 g carbohydrates; 2.8 g fiber; 181 mg sodium. 8 servings.

Dare Reich, former staff and Friend of Lewisville Library

"The best of all physicians
Is apple pie and cheese!"

Eugene Field, 1850-1895
Apple Pie and Cheese

French Cherry Pie

3 oz. cream cheese, softened
$^2/_3$ c. confectioner's sugar
1 c. whipping cream
1 pie shell, baked
21-oz. can cherry pie filling

Mix softened cream cheese with sugar. Add cream. Whip until stiff. Spoon mixture into baked pie shell. Using fork, put pie filling on top of whipped cream mixture. Chill. Note: I like to use Betty Crocker® pie crust mix, adding chopped almonds.

Nutrition facts per serving: 380 calories; 1.6 g protein; 21.8 g fat; 44.1 g carbohydrates; 0.5 g fiber; 166 mg sodium. 8 servings.

Elizabeth Skinner, current staff

Frozen Lemonade Pie

1¾ c. cold milk
2 pkgs. instant vanilla pudding mix
6-oz. can frozen lemonade concentrate, thawed
8 oz. Cool Whip® whipped topping, thawed
1 graham cracker pie crust
lemon or kiwi slices (optional)

Pour milk into large bowl. Add pudding mix and whisk or beat well for 30 seconds. Add lemonade concentrate and whisk or beat 30 seconds more. Mixture will be thick. Stir in Cool Whip® and spoon into pie crust. Refrigerate for 4 hours or until set. Garnish with lemon or kiwi slices if desired. Refrigerate or freeze any leftovers.

Nutrition facts per serving: 405 calories; 3.5 g protein; 13.9 g fat; 65.8 g carbohydrates; 0.7 g fiber; 551 mg sodium. 8 servings.

A cool and delicious dessert for hot summer days!
Wendy Riedel Bright, sister of staff member and officer at Forsyth County Detention Center

Strawberry Pie

1 c. water
½ c. granulated sugar
¼ tsp. salt
2 Tbsp. cornstarch
1 pkg. strawberry flavor Jell-O® gelatin
1 qt. sliced strawberries
1 pie shell, baked

Combine water, sugar, salt and cornstarch in medium saucepan. Cook and stir until mixture is thick and clear. Remove from heat and add Jell-O®. Let cool. Put strawberries in baked pie shell. Pour glaze over berries and refrigerate. May be served with whipped cream or Cool Whip® whipped topping.

Nutrition facts per serving: 210 calories; 2.3 g protein; 5.6 g fat; 39.4 g carbohydrates; 2.1 g fiber; 208 mg sodium. 8 servings.

Judy Prater, current staff

Million Dollar Pie

12 oz. Cool Whip® whipped topping, thawed
20-oz. can crushed juice-pack pineapple, drained
14-oz. can sweetened condensed milk
½ c. chopped nuts
¼ c. lemon juice
2 pie shells, baked
½ c. shredded coconut
10-oz. jar maraschino cherries, drained and chopped

Mix together Cool Whip®, pineapple, condensed milk, nuts and lemon juice. Pour into baked pie shells. Top with coconut and cherries. Chill at least 4 hours.

Nutrition facts per serving: 303 calories; 3.0 g protein; 14.2 g fat; 39.5 g carbohydrates; 1.3 g fiber; 140 mg sodium. 16 servings (2 pies).

Gladys Edwards, former staff

Jennifer's Favorite Pumpkin Pie

2 eggs, slightly beaten
1¾ c. (1 can) cooked or canned pumpkin
¾ c. granulated sugar
½ tsp. pumpkin pie spice
¼ tsp. ground cinnamon
¼ tsp. ground ginger
1½ cans (2¼ c.) evaporated milk
1 tsp. vanilla extract
1 unbaked 9" deep-dish pie shell

Preheat oven to 400ºF. Combine filling ingredients in order given. Pour into pie crust. Bake for 10 minutes, then reduce heat to 350ºF and bake for another 45 minutes or until knife inserted in center comes out clean. Cool.

Nutrition facts per serving: 279 calories; 4.6 g protein; 11.2 g fat; 40.2 g carbohydrates; 1.6 g fiber; 166 mg sodium. 8 servings.

This is my absolute favorite pie, which my mom makes without a recipe! I had to make her let me write down all the ingredients and measurements so I would have this recipe for myself to bake.
Jennifer Wiseman, Friend of the Lewisville Library

"I ate umble pie with an appetite."

Charles Dickens, 1812-1870
David Copperfield

Mrs. Williams's Pumpkin Pie

2 c. cooked pumpkin
¾ of 16-oz. tub Betty Crocker® coconut pecan frosting
1 tsp. pumpkin pie spice
½ tsp. salt
3 Tbsp. all-purpose flour
2½ c. granulated sugar
2 eggs
$^{2}/_{3}$ stick ($^{1}/_{3}$ c.) butter, melted
1 tsp. vanilla extract
¾ c. milk
2 unbaked pie shells
2 Tbsp. brown sugar

Preheat oven to 375°F. Combine all ingredients except pie shells and brown sugar and mix well. Pour equal amounts into each pie shell and sprinkle with brown sugar. Place pies on cookie sheets to ensure crusts cook evenly. Bake for 15 minutes. Then reduce heat to 325°F and bake for 35 to 45 minutes or until set. Note: Whipped cream topping adds to perfection.

Nutrition facts per serving: 361 calories; 2.5 g protein; 14.4 g fat; 56.0 g carbohydrates; 1.6 g fiber; 264 mg sodium. 16 servings (2 pies).

While most Southerners love sweet potato pie, this pumpkin pie was always a surprise hit and often rivaled sweet potato pies wherever my mother took it. I'm not sure where she got the recipe, but the coconut pecan frosting gives it a traditional candied sweet potato pie touch.
Melisa Williams, current staff. "This recipe is submitted in memory of my mother, Violet Elizabeth Williams, a great cook and lover of books. She taught us to read before we started school. She also read to us every night before bedtime. She now has two daughters and a granddaughter who are librarians."

Grandmother Wheeless's Pumpkin Pie

1¾ c. (1 can) cooked pumpkin
¼ c. granulated sugar
½ tsp. salt
1 tsp. ground cinnamon
½ tsp. ground ginger
1/8 tsp. ground cloves
2 eggs
1½ c. (12-oz. can) evaporated milk
¼ c. molasses
1 tsp. vanilla extract
1 unbaked pie shell

Preheat oven to 450ºF. Turn pumpkin into saucepan and cook over direct heat for 10 minutes until somewhat dry and slightly caramelized, stirring constantly. Remove from heat. Blend sugar, salt and spices and stir into hot pumpkin. Beat eggs, evaporated milk, molasses and vanilla together and beat into pumpkin mixture until smooth. Pour into pie shell and bake 15 minutes. Reduce heat to 300ºF and bake about 45 minutes longer or until knife inserted in center comes out clean.

Nutrition facts per serving: 207 calories; 4.5 g protein; 8.4 g fat; 29.2 g carbohydrates; 1.9 g fiber; 295 mg sodium. 8 servings.

This recipe is from my husband's grandmother.
Kathleen Wheeless, current staff

Sweet Potato Pie

2 eggs
1 c. granulated sugar
1 tsp. salt
¼ tsp. ground nutmeg
1 tsp. ground cinnamon
1 c. milk
2 med. sweet potatoes, cooked, peeled and mashed through ricer (about 1½ c.)
2 Tbsp. butter, melted
1 unbaked 9" pie shell

Preheat oven to 450ºF. Beat eggs slightly in medium bowl. Add sugar, salt, spices and milk and stir. In small bowl, mix sweet potatoes with butter. Blend sweet potato mixture into milk and egg mixture. Pour into unbaked pie shell. Bake for 10 minutes, then reduce heat to 350ºF and bake for another 30 to 40 minutes or until filling is firm.

Nutrition facts per serving: 315 calories; 3.3 g protein; 12.3 g fat; 47.6 g carbohydrates; 1.5 g fiber; 475 mg sodium. 8 servings.

This recipe comes from my mother.
Rob Norwood, current staff

Satia's Sweet Potato Pie

1 unbaked deep dish pie shell
2 c. mashed cooked sweet potatoes
2 eggs, beaten (Egg Beaters® are OK)
1¼ c. milk (low-fat is OK)
¾ c. granulated sugar (can substitute some with brown sugar or artificial sweetener)
½ tsp. salt or to taste
½+ tsp. cinnamon
½+ tsp. nutmeg (freshly grated is best)
2+ Tbsp. bourbon
4 Tbsp. butter, melted
dash vanilla extract

Preheat oven to 425ºF. Par-bake pie shell for 5 to 10 minutes to prevent it from sticking. Combine all other ingredients. Beat until smooth and pour into crust. Dust top with additional nutmeg. Bake 10 minutes at 425ºF then reduce heat to 325ºF and bake for about 50 minutes or until filling is firm, which is usually longer. Notes: You can boil or bake potatoes. I sometimes feel baking gives a deeper flavor. Do not skimp on the spices and bourbon!

Nutrition facts per serving: 344 calories; 3.8 g protein; 15.5 g fat; 44.7 g carbohydrates; 1.9 g fiber; 369 mg sodium. 8 servings.

Adapted from Fanny Farmer Cookbook *and inspired by Satia Orange, a former staff member, emphasizing liberal booze use for flavor.*
Dave Fergusson, current staff

"You have baked me too brown, I must sugar my hair."

Lewis Carroll, 1832-1898
Alice's Adventures in Wonderland

Coconut Pie

1 c. shredded coconut
milk (approx. ¾ c.)
3 eggs
1 c. granulated sugar
1 stick (½ c.) butter, melted
1 tsp. vanilla extract
½ tsp. salt
1 unbaked 9" pie shell

Preheat oven to 350ºF. While coconut is in measuring cup, pour in enough milk to cover and set aside. In mixing bowl, beat eggs. Add sugar, butter, vanilla and salt and beat well. Add coconut and milk and stir. Pour into unbaked pie shell and bake until light brown, at least 45 minutes.

Nutrition facts per serving: 254 calories; 2.8 g protein; 15.6 g fat; 26.5 g carbohydrates; 0.5 g fiber; 287 mg sodium. 12 servings.

This recipe came from my mother. This pie has been enjoyed at many library staff get-togethers.
Rob Norwood, current staff

Chocolate Chess Pie

2 squares unsweetened chocolate
2 c. granulated sugar
1 Tbsp. corn meal
1 Tbsp. all-purpose flour
4 eggs
3 Tbsp. butter, melted
¼ c. milk
1 unbaked pie shell

Preheat oven to 350°F. Melt chocolate in double boiler over, not in, boiling water. In large bowl, mix sugar, corn meal and flour. Add eggs 1 at a time and beat well after each addition. Stir in melted butter, milk and chocolate and mix well. Pour mixture into pie shell. Bake for 35 to 45 minutes or until firm. You may wish to cover pie with foil tent after 30 minutes. Cool before cutting.

Nutrition facts per serving: 292 calories; 2.8 g protein; 12.2 g fat; 44.9 g carbohydrates; 0.7 g fiber; 127 mg sodium. 12 servings.

All my good pie recipes come from my mom.
Rob Norwood, current staff

Pecan Pie

¾ c. granulated sugar
1 Tbsp. cornmeal
3 eggs
1 c. dark Karo® corn syrup (blue label)
1/8 tsp. salt
2 Tbsp. butter, melted
1 tsp. vanilla extract
½ c. chopped pecans
9″ unbaked pie shell, deep-dish preferred
pecan halves to place on top

Preheat oven to 425°F. Have all ingredients ready before your start. Mix sugar and cornmeal. Lightly beat eggs and add sugar mixture. Add corn syrup, salt, butter, vanilla and chopped pecans. Pour into pie shell. Top with pecan halves. Bake at 425°F for 10 minutes only. Reduce heat to 325°F and bake for 30 to 35 minutes longer. Do not open oven door before 30 minutes. Top with vanilla ice cream, if desired.

Nutrition facts per serving: 277 calories; 2.0 g protein; 11.2 g fat; 43.9 g carbohydrates; 0.5 g fiber; 175 mg sodium. 12 servings.

Barbara Rickert, Friend of Reynolda Library

COOKIES & BROWNIES

Banana Oatmeal Cookies

3 c. all-purpose flour
2 c. granulated sugar
2 tsp. baking soda
1 tsp. salt
1½ tsp. ground cinnamon
1 c. vegetable oil
2 c. very ripe bananas, mashed
2 whole eggs
3½ c. rolled oats (not quick-cooking kind)
1 c. nuts, chopped
1 c. raisins or dried cranberries

Preheat oven to 375°F. Mix flour, sugar, baking soda, salt and cinnamon together. Add oil, bananas, eggs, oats, nuts and raisins or dried cranberries. Mix well. Drop by heaping tablespoonful on cookie sheet. Bake approximately 12 minutes. Note: For a healthier version, I substitute ½ cup all-purpose flour with whole wheat flour, ½ cup sugar with Splenda® artificial sweetener and ½ cup oil with applesauce.

Nutrition facts per cookie (original version): 86 calories; 1.2 g protein; 3.8 g fat; 12.2 g carbohydrates; 0.6 g fiber; 60 mg sodium.
Per serving (healthier version): 67 calories; 1.1 g protein; 2.5 g fat; 10.3 g carbohydrates; 0.7 g fiber; 60 mg sodium.
7 dozen cookies.

My aunt Vye gave me this recipe. With the substitutions in the note, I feel this is a healthy and delicious treat—and so good!
Ramona Litcher, Friend of Lewisville Library. "I love to read!! And I am so excited about the new library that is soon to be under construction!"

Oatmeal Walnut Cookies

1½ c. all-purpose flour
1 tsp. salt
1 Tbsp. baking soda
3 c. rolled oats
½ c. chopped walnuts
1 c. shortening
1 c. granulated sugar
1 c. packed brown sugar
2 eggs
1 tsp. vanilla extract

Sift flour, salt and baking soda together. Stir in oats and nuts. Set aside. Cream shortening and sugars. Add eggs and vanilla and mix. Add dry ingredients and mix thoroughly. You may refrigerate dough overnight if desired. To bake, preheat oven to 350°F. Drop dough by teaspoonful on ungreased cookie sheet. Bake for 10 to 12 minutes. Note: You may use pecans or macadamia nuts if you prefer.

Nutrition facts per cookie: 85 calories; 1.0 g protein; 4.4 g fat; 10.7 g carbohydrates; 0.3 g fiber; 105 mg sodium. 5 dozen cookies.

Carol Brown, Board member of Friends of Reynolda Manor Library. "I read a lot and am one of the library's most enthusiastic patrons."

Old Fashioned Oatmeal Cookies

1 c. raisins
1 c. water
¾ c. shortening
1½ c. granulated sugar
2 eggs
1 tsp. vanilla extract
2½ c. self-rising flour
1 tsp. ground cinnamon
½ tsp. ground cloves
2 c. quick-cooking oats
½ c. nuts, chopped
¼ c. packed brown sugar

Preheat oven to 400ºF. Simmer raisins and water over medium heat until raisins are plump (about 15 minutes). Drain raisins, reserving liquid. Add enough water to reserved liquid to measure ½ cup. Thoroughly mix shortening, sugar, eggs and vanilla. Stir in reserved liquid. Blend in remaining ingredients. Drop dough by rounded tablespoonfuls about 2 inches apart onto ungreased baking sheets. Bake 8 to 10 minutes or until light brown. Makes ugly, yet delicious, cookies.

Nutrition facts per cookie: 142 calories; 1.9 g protein; 5.8 g fat; 21.2 g carbohydrates; 0.8 g fiber; 115 mg sodium. 3 dozen cookies.

This is my favorite recipe from my mother's kitchen
Matt Shaw, current staff

"Think what a better world it would be if we all, the whole world, had cookies and milk about three o'clock every afternoon and then lay down on our blankets for a nap."

Barbara Jordan, 1936-1996

Indian Boiled Cookies

2 Tbsp. unsweetened cocoa powder
2 c. granulated sugar
½ c. milk
1 stick (½ c.) margarine
½ c. peanut butter (creamy or chunky)
3 c. quick-cooking oats
1 tsp. vanilla extract
dash salt

Mix cocoa, sugar and milk in small saucepan. Bring to boil and cook 1 minute. Remove from heat and stir in remaining ingredients. Drop onto wax paper. Let stand until firm.

Nutrition facts per cookie: 153 calories; 2.4 g protein; 7.0 g fat; 21.4 g carbohydrates; 1.0 g fiber; 72 mg sodium. 2 dozen cookies.

Valena V. Vogler, former staff

Sesame Cookies

2 c. all-purpose flour
½ tsp. baking powder
2 eggs, divided
1 stick (½ c.) butter, melted
½ c. granulated sugar
1 Tbsp. water
3 Tbsp. sesame seeds

Preheat oven to 350°F. Sift flour and baking soda into bowl. Beat 1 egg. Make hollow in center of flour mixture and pour in melted butter, sugar and beaten egg. Work mixture together until soft dough is formed. Add small amount of water if necessary. Knead gently until smooth. Turn out on lightly floured board. Shape into ½" roll. Cut roll into ½" pieces and roll them into balls. Press balls flat on greased cookie sheet. Separate remaining egg. Beat yolk with 1 tablespoon water. Beat egg white in separate bowl. Brush cookies lightly with egg yolk mixture. Sprinkle cookies with sesame seeds, then brush with beaten egg white. Bake 15 to 20 minutes or until brown.

Nutrition facts per cookie: 40 calories; 0.8 g protein; 1.9 g fat; 4.9 g carbohydrates; 0.2 g fiber; 22 mg sodium. 5 dozen cookies.

Gerry Eggleston, former staff
Editor's note: My South Carolina grandmother used to call these Benne Wafers. They're small, elegant and not too sweet. They may also be rolled and cut instead of being shaped by hand.

Peanut Butter Chocolate Chip Cookies

2 sticks (1 c.) butter, softened
1 c. peanut butter, creamy or chunky
1 c. granulated sugar
1 c. packed brown sugar
2 eggs, beaten
2 c. all-purpose flour
1 tsp. baking soda
6-oz. pkg. semi-sweet chocolate chips

Preheat oven to 325°F. In large bowl, beat butter and peanut butter together. Add both types of sugar and stir. Add eggs and mix. Add flour and baking soda and mix well. Stir in chocolate chips. Drop by spoonfuls onto ungreased cookie sheet. Bake 12 to 15 minutes.

Nutrition facts per cookie: 92 calories; 1.6 g protein; 5.2 g fat; 10.6 g carbohydrates; 0.4 g fiber; 63 mg sodium. 6 dozen cookies.

This recipe came from my mother, Betty Avery Norwood.
Rob Norwood, current staff

> "Me want cookie!"
>
> Cookie Monster, timeless
> *Sesame Street*

Dena Southard's Ginger Snaps

- ¾ c. shortening
- 1 c. packed brown sugar
- ¼ c. molasses
- 1 egg
- 2 c. all-purpose flour
- ¼ tsp. salt
- 2 tsp. baking soda
- 1 tsp. ground cinnamon
- 1 tsp. ground cloves
- 1 tsp. ground ginger
- ½ c. granulated sugar

Preheat oven to 375ºF. Cream shortening and sugar together. Add molasses and egg. Sift flour, salt, baking soda and spices together and add to creamed mixture. Roll dough into 1" balls and then roll in granulated sugar. Place on ungreased cookie sheet and bake 8 to 10 minutes.

Nutrition facts per cookie: 45 calories; 0.4 g protein; 1.9 g fat; 6.8 g carbohydrates; 0.1 g fiber; 39 mg sodium. 7 dozen cookies.

From a freshman year dorm-mate. These cookies made late night study sessions more bearable.
Lise Keppler, current staff

Marcia Bernsten's English Toffee Cookies

- 2 eggs, separated
- 2 sticks (1 c.) butter, softened
- 1 c. granulated sugar
- 2 c. cake flour
- 1 tsp. salt
- 1 tsp. cinnamon
- 1 tsp. vanilla extract
- 1 c. pecans, finely chopped

Preheat oven to 375ºF. Beat egg whites until frothy. In large bowl, cream butter and sugar together. Add egg yolks and beat. Sift flour, salt and cinnamon together and add to creamed mixture. Mix well. Add vanilla and ½ cup pecans. Mix well. Press dough into greased jelly roll pan or rimmed cookie sheet (10"x15"). Spread beaten egg whites over dough and sprinkle with remaining nuts. Bake for 30 minutes. Cut while still warm.

Nutrition facts per cookie: 90 calories; 1.0 g protein; 5.7 g fat; 9.0 g carbohydrates; 0.3 g fiber; 90 mg sodium. 4 dozen cookies.

Roommates more than 30 years ago and still friends!
Lise Keppler, current staff

Butterscotch Brownies

¾ c. butter or margarine
2 c. packed light brown sugar
1 c. all-purpose flour
1 tsp. salt
2 eggs, lightly beaten
2 tsp. vanilla extract
1 c. broken pecans or walnuts
1 Tbsp. confectioner's sugar

Preheat oven to 350ºF. Melt butter in heavy skillet over low heat. Add sugar and stir until blended and smooth. Add flour and salt and stir until smooth. Remove from heat. Cool 4 or 5 minutes. Add eggs and vanilla. Pour into greased 9"x9" baking pan. Bake 30 minutes or until brownies test done. (May feel sticky to touch.) Sprinkle with confectioner's sugar while still warm. Cool and cut into 1" squares but leave in pan for several hours until completely cold. Will keep well in air-tight container for week or more.

Nutrition facts per brownie: 238 calories; 2.0 g protein; 12.6 g fat; 30.5 g carbohydrates; 0.7 g fiber; 224 mg sodium. 18 brownies.

From Emily Williams, former staff member.
Elizabeth Skinner, current staff

Strong Girl Brownies

1 stick (½ c.) butter
1 lb. dark brown sugar
2 eggs
2 tsp. vanilla extract
1 c. all-purpose flour
1 tsp. salt
2 tsp. baking powder
2 c. finely chopped pecans
1 Tbsp. (approx.) confectioner's sugar

Preheat oven to 350ºF. Grease 9"x13" baking pan. Melt butter in 3-quart saucepan over low heat. Remove from heat and stir in brown sugar. Let cool slightly and beat in eggs and vanilla. Stir in flour, salt and baking powder. Add pecans last. Spread into greased pan. Bake for 25 to 30 minutes until done. Let cool slightly. Sprinkle with confectioner's sugar and cut into small squares. Notes: These are much easier to cut while they are still slightly warm. This recipe could not be easier. There's only one saucepan to clean up!

Nutrition facts per brownie: 217 calories; 1.9 g protein; 10.8 g fat; 30.0 g carbohydrates; 1.0 g fiber; 192 mg sodium. 24 brownies.

In some corners, this is known as the "Official Recipe of Quiz Bowl!"
Cal Shepard, former staff and Manager of Consortial Outreach, SOLINET (Southeastern Library Network)

Turtle Brownies

14 oz. caramels
14-oz. can sweetened condensed milk
1½ sticks (¾ c.) butter, melted
1 box chocolate or German chocolate cake mix
1 c. chopped pecans
12 oz. chocolate chips, divided
1 Tbsp. milk

Preheat oven to 350ºF. Unwrap caramels. In saucepan over low heat, melt caramels with ½ can of condensed milk and set aside. Mix melted butter, remaining condensed milk, cake mix and ½ cup pecans together. Place half of batter in greased 9"x13" pan and bake for 6 minutes. Sprinkle 1 cup chocolate chips over top, then remaining nuts. Pour caramel mixture over nuts and chocolate chips. Mix milk into remaining batter. In small amounts, press batter in hands and place over caramel. Sprinkle remaining chocolate chips over top and bake for 15 minutes more.

Nutrition facts per brownie: 355 calories; 4.2 g protein; 19.1 g fat; 46.6 g carbohydrates; 1.9 g fiber; 300 mg sodium. 24 brownies.

Came from my mom about 22 years ago in one of her experimental moments.
Jacquelyn Smith, current staff
Editor's note: Jacque's brownies have been used as library staff incentives more than once!

Summit Lemon Squares

2 sticks (1 c.) butter, softened
2 c. all-purpose flour
½ c. confectioner's sugar

Filling

4 eggs, beaten
2 c. granulated sugar
6 Tbsp. lemon juice
1 Tbsp. all-purpose flour
½ tsp. baking powder
1 c. chopped pecans

Preheat oven to 325ºF. Combine butter, flour and confectioner's sugar to form pastry. Press into 9"x13" baking pan. Bake for 15 minutes and remove from oven. Combine filling ingredients and pour over pastry. Bake for another 40 to 50 minutes. May be sprinkled with confectioner's sugar if desired.

Nutrition facts per square: 224 calories; 2.6 g protein; 11.8 g fat; 28.1 g carbohydrates; 0.7 g fiber; 99 mg sodium. 24 squares.

From Emily Williams, former staff member.
Elizabeth Skinner, current staff

Lemon Bars

3 eggs, divided
$^{2}/_{3}$ stick ($^{1}/_{3}$ c.) butter, softened
1 box lemon cake mix
1 c. granulated sugar
½ tsp. baking powder
¼ tsp. salt
2 Tbsp. grated lemon rind
¼ c. lemon juice
1 Tbsp. (approx.) confectioner's sugar

Preheat oven to 350ºF. Mix 1 egg, butter and cake mix until crumbly. Reserve 1 cup of mixture. Pat remaining cake mixture lightly into 9"x13" pan. Bake 15 minutes or until lightly browned. Meanwhile, beat remaining eggs, sugar, baking powder, salt, lemon rind and lemon juice together until light and foamy. Pour over hot crust. Crumble reserved cake mixture on top. Bake 15 minutes or until lightly browned. Sprinkle with confectioner's sugar.

Nutrition facts per bar: 161 calories; 1.7 g protein; 5.7 g fat; 26.1 g carbohydrates; 0.4 g fiber; 212 mg sodium. 24 bars.

Vivian Taylor, former staff

OTHER SWEETS

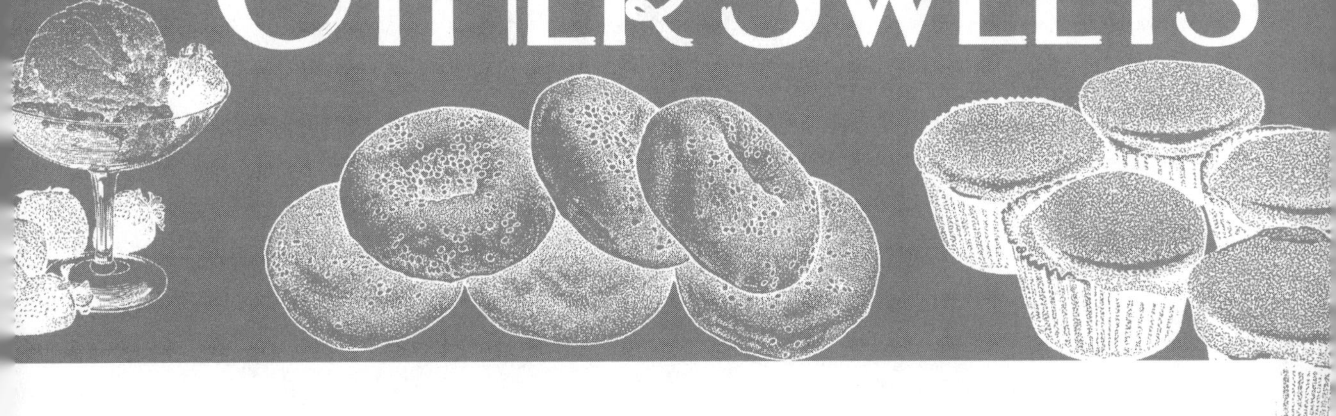

Easy Rice Pudding 'Comfort Food'

4½ c. milk, divided
½ c. granulated sugar
½ c. Uncle Ben's® converted white rice
1 egg
1 tsp. vanilla extract
1 tsp. almond extract (optional)
ground cinnamon to taste

In medium saucepan, blend 4 cups milk with sugar and rice. Bring to boil, cover and simmer over low heat for 1 hour. Stir occasionally to prevent milk from boiling over. When rice has cooked, beat egg. Add ½ cup milk and vanilla (and almond extract if desired) to egg and mix well. Add egg and milk mixture to saucepan. Return to boil and cook 2 to 3 minutes. Pour into serving bowl and cool. Sprinkle with cinnamon and serve.

Nutrition facts per serving: 186 calories; 6.3 g protein; 5.1 g fat; 26.4 g carbohydrates; 0 g fiber; 76 mg sodium. 8 servings.

This recipe came from friends in New York state. I often add raisins.
Mary Tucker, volunteer and Friend of the Library. "There are so many interesting things to look at. Try the juvenile nonfiction sometime, even if you're far from being a juvenile!"

Banana Pudding

2 boxes instant vanilla pudding mix
3 c. milk
8 oz. Cool Whip® whipped topping, thawed
8 oz. sour cream
12-oz. box vanilla wafers
3 bananas, sliced

Mix pudding, milk, Cool Whip® and sour cream. Make layer of vanilla wafers in bottom of casserole dish. Cover with half of bananas, followed by half of pudding mixture. Repeat layers. Crush a few of remaining vanilla wafers and sprinkle on top. (You'll probably have some vanilla wafers left over.) Chill and serve. Notes: To make this recipe less fattening, use fat-free, sugar-free pudding mix, skim milk, fat-free Cool Whip®, fat-free sour cream and reduced fat vanilla wafers. It's quite good! For variety, use sliced strawberries instead of bananas.

Nutrition facts per serving: 482 calories; 5.6 g protein; 20.7 g fat; 68.6 g carbohydrates; 1.1 g fiber; 540 mg sodium. 8 servings.

Vicki Taylor, current staff

Mocha Charlottes

1 pkg. unflavored gelatin
¼ c. cold water
½ c. granulated sugar
2 eggs
1 c. milk
⅓ c. semisweet chocolate chips
1½ tsp. instant coffee granules
2 tsp. vanilla extract
1 c. whipping cream
2 3-oz. pkgs. ladyfingers, split
3 Tbsp. confectioner's sugar

Sprinkle gelatin over cold water, stir and let stand 1 minute. Set aside. Beat sugar and eggs at medium speed until thick and pale, about 2 to 3 minutes. Heat milk in large saucepan over low heat. Gradually add about ¼ of milk to egg mixture. Add remaining hot milk, stirring constantly. Return mixture to saucepan and cook over low heat, stirring constantly, until mixture coats spoon, about 4 to 5 minutes. Remove from heat. Stir in gelatin mixture until gelatin dissolves. Whisk in chocolate chips, coffee granules and vanilla until coffee dissolves and chocolate melts. Pour mixture into metal bowl sitting in ice and let stand, stirring often, 6 to 8 minutes or until cold and slightly thickened. Beat whipping cream on high speed until soft peaks form. Fold whipped cream into mocha mixture. Line each of 8 teacups with 6 ladyfinger halves, placing rounded sides of ladyfingers against edge of each cup. Spoon custard evenly into cups, cover and chill 8 hours.

Nutrition facts per serving: 347 calories; 5.9 g protein; 22.3 g fat; 32.8 g carbohydrates; 0.4 g fiber; 72 mg sodium. 8 servings.

Served at On The Same Page program featuring To Kill a Mockingbird *by Harper Lee.*
Merrikay Brown, current staff

Persimmon Pudding

1 c. persimmon pulp
1 c. granulated sugar
1½ c. all-purpose flour
2 tsp. baking powder
1 tsp. salt
2 eggs
1 stick (½ c.) melted butter
1 c. sweet milk

Preheat oven to 375°F. Mix all ingredients in order given. Pour into lightly greased 8" x 11" baking pan. Bake for 30-40 minutes. (Editor's note: Persimmon pulp is available at local farmers' markets when in season and may be found in some specialty food stores. Or you can make your own by peeling ripe persimmons and pressing fruit through strainer.)

Nutrition facts per serving: 249 calories; 3.7 g protein; 9.3 g fat; 38.9 g carbohydrates; 2.1 g fiber; 375 mg sodium. 12 servings.

My husband Tom makes this from his mother's old cookbook, Concord Presbyterian Church Cookbook, *from Statesville, NC.*
Merrikay Brown, current staff

Sweet Potato Dumplings

1 med. cooked sweet potato, peeled
12-oz. can refrigerated biscuits
1 c. granulated sugar
1 c. water
1 stick (½ c.) butter
ground cinnamon to taste
vanilla extract to taste

Preheat oven to 350°F. Slice sweet potato ¼" thick. Roll out canned biscuits and put one slice of sweet potato in middle of each one. Crimp dough to center of potato and seal with fork. Place filled biscuits in baking dish. In saucepan, combine remaining ingredients. Heat mixture, stirring constantly. Pour hot syrup over dumplings. Bake until brown. Cover dish with foil and return it to oven for few more minutes to allow syrup to thicken.

Nutrition facts per serving: 288 calories; 2.4 g protein; 13.7 g fat; 39.0 g carbohydrates; 0.6 g fiber; 461 mg sodium. 10 servings.

Vivian Taylor, former staff

Peach Praline Cobbler

1 qt. sliced fresh peaches
1¾ c. granulated sugar, divided
ground cinnamon to taste
1¾ c. self-rising flour
1 c. milk
1 egg, well beaten

Topping

½ stick (4 Tbsp.) margarine
¾ c. self-rising flour
1½ c. pecans, coarsely chopped
⅓ c. packed light brown sugar

Preheat oven to 350°F. Place peaches in bowl, sprinkle with ¼ cup sugar and cinnamon. Set aside for a few minutes and strain off excess juice. Combine remaining batter ingredients and mix well. Pour into well greased 9"x13" pan. Arrange peaches evenly on top of batter. Prepare topping by cutting margarine into small pieces and allowing it to come up to room temperature. Using spoon or pastry blender, mix in other topping ingredients until crumbly. Sprinkle topping evenly over peaches. Bake for 70 minutes and serve warm with vanilla ice cream.

Nutrition facts per serving: 240 calories; 3.3 g protein; 5.7 g fat; 44.9 g carbohydrates; 1.6 g fiber; 271 mg sodium. 16 servings.

This is an old South Carolina recipe.
Thomasina Hawkins, Friend of Lewisville Library

> "The proof of the pudding is in the eating."
>
> Miguel de Cervantes, 1547-1616
> *Don Quixote de la Mancha*

Toffee or Pecan Pastries

3 oz. cream cheese, softened
1 stick (½ c.) butter, softened
1 c. sifted all-purpose flour

Filling

¾ c. packed brown sugar
1 Tbsp. butter, melted
¼ tsp. salt
½ tsp. vanilla extract
1 egg, beaten
½ c. chopped pecans (optional)

Blend cream cheese, butter and flour thoroughly and chill. To make pastries, preheat oven to 350ºF. Pinch off 24 balls of dough and press into tiny muffin pans to form cups. In saucepan, blend brown sugar, butter, salt, vanilla and egg and heat. Spoon filling into unbaked shells. Sprinkle pecans on top if desired. Bake for 25 minutes.

Nutrition facts per serving (without pecans): 99 calories; 1.1 g protein; 5.8 g fat; 10.8 g carbohydrates; 0.1 g fiber; 84 mg sodium.
Per serving (with pecans): 114 calories; 1.3 g protein; 7.5 g fat; 11.1 g carbohydrates; 0.3 g fiber; 84 mg sodium.
24 servings.

Served at On The Same Page program featuring To Kill a Mockingbird *by Harper Lee.*
Merrikay Brown, current staff

French Vanilla Ice Cream

3 eggs
2 c. milk
1 c. granulated sugar
2 c. heavy cream
2 tsp. vanilla extract

Beat eggs and milk together in large saucepan. Add sugar. Cook over low heat, stirring constantly, until thickened (approximately 10 minutes). Mixture should smoothly coat spoon. Cool, then add cream and vanilla. Refrigerate overnight. Next day, freeze mixture in ice cream freezer, following manufacturer's directions.

Nutrition facts per serving: 371 calories; 5.5 g protein; 25.9 g fat; 30.1 g carbohydrates; 0 g fiber; 76 mg sodium. 8 servings.

Juanita A. Tatum, Forsyth County Public Library Board of Trustees

Mother's Ice Cream Crunch

6 c. Special K® cereal
½ c. margarine, melted
⅔ c. granulated sugar
1 c. coconut
½ gallon favorite ice cream, softened

Crush cereal in plastic bag using rolling pin. (You can double the cereal for extra thick crunch.) Add margarine, sugar and coconut into cereal bag and mix. Place half of mixture in bottom of 9"x13" dish. Add softened ice cream and top with remaining crunch mixture. Freeze and cut in squares to serve. Notes: Can be served with hot fudge topping or chocolate syrup. I usually cut away carton from ice cream, put on cutting board and slice. Neapolitan ice cream makes a pretty combination. We also use coffee and chocolate combination often.

Nutrition facts per serving: 293 calories; 5.5 g protein; 14.8 g fat; 38.4 g carbohydrates; 0.6 g fiber; 219 mg sodium. 16 servings.

This was served in my home as long as I can remember and now my children and grandchildren request it when they come on holidays.
Mitzi Loflin Sapp, Friend of Clemmons Library

Fruit and Angel Dessert

1 large (14-oz.) angel food cake
15-oz. can crushed juice-pack pineapple, not drained
10-oz. jar maraschino cherries, drained and chopped
12 oz. Cool Whip® whipped topping, thawed
3½-oz. can flaked coconut, toasted

Break cake into bite-sized pieces. Arrange half of cake pieces in bottom of 9"x13" baking dish. Top with half of pineapple and half of cherries. Spread half of Cool Whip® over this and top with half of coconut. Repeat layers, ending with Cool Whip® and coconut. Refrigerate for several hours or overnight.

Nutrition facts per serving: 273 calories; 1.6 g protein; 7.5 g fat; 46.3 g carbohydrates; 1.2 g fiber; 341 mg sodium. 12 servings.

This was found in a large bag of recipes I bought at the Antique Mall in Galax, VA. Some lady that had evidently passed on had clippings from magazines and old newspapers stuffed in the bag, which was sold for $1.00!
Mitzi Loflin Sapp, Friend of Clemmons Library

Granny's Cherry Yum-Yum

3 c. graham cracker crumbs
1½ sticks (¾ c.) margarine, melted
2 (2.6-oz.) pkg. Dream Whip® topping mix
1 c. cold milk
¾ c. granulated sugar
8 oz. cream cheese, softened
21-oz. can cherry pie filling (or other flavor)

Mix graham cracker crumbs and margarine. Reserve ½ cup of mixture. Form crust by pressing remaining mixture into 9"x13" baking dish. Combine Dream Whip® and milk and beat well. Add sugar and cream cheese and blend. Spread half of cream cheese mixture over crust. Pour pie filling on top. Spread remaining cream cheese mixture over pie filling. Sprinkle with reserved crumbs and chill for 2 hours.

Nutrition facts per serving: 353 calories; 3.6 g protein; 38.6 g fat; 45.0 g carbohydrates; 0.9 g fiber; 287 mg sodium. 15 servings.

My Granny always took this dish to all our church gatherings and just called it Yum-Yum.
Judy Fishel Joyce, member Forsyth County Public Library Board of Trustees

Peach Delight

1 stick (½ c.) margarine, softened or melted
½ c. finely chopped nuts
1 c. all-purpose flour
1¼ c. +2 Tbsp. granulated sugar, divided
8 oz. cream cheese, softened
1 c. confectioner's sugar
12 oz. Cool Whip® whipped topping, thawed and divided
3 c. sliced fresh peaches
2 c. water
3 Tbsp. cornstarch
1 pkg. peach flavor Jell-O® gelatin

Preheat oven to 350°F. To make Layer 1, mix margarine, nuts, flour and 2 Tbsp. granulated sugar. Spread in greased 9"x13" pan and bake for 15 minutes. Cool completely. For Layer 2, cream together cream cheese and confectioner's sugar. Fold in half of Cool Whip®. Spread on cooled crust and chill. For Layer 3, arrange sliced peaches over chilled cream cheese mixture. For Layer 4, combine water, 1¼ cup granulated sugar and cornstarch in saucepan. Cook over low to medium heat until clear, stirring constantly. Add Jell-O and mix well. Let this glaze cool, then pour on top of peaches. Chill completely. For Layer 5, top with remaining Cool Whip®.

Variation: For Lemon Delight, replace Layer 3 with 2 pkgs. lemon pudding and pie filling prepared according to package directions and skip Layer 4.

Nutrition facts per serving: 350 calories; 3.0 g protein; 16.8 g fat; 46.7 g carbohydrates; 1.2 g fiber; 117 mg sodium. 16 servings.

This recipe was shared by my mother's first cousin's wife at a family reunion in August 1984. It was a popular dish. Donna L. Staley, Chairman of the Forsyth County Public Library Board of Trustees. "I am so thankful for the open doors of unlimited knowledge available at the library."

"But thou wast up by break of day,
And brought'st Thy sweets along with Thee."

George Herbert, 1593-1633
Easter

Peach Delight with Pineapple

2 pkg. peach flavor Jell-O® gelatin
8-oz. can crushed juice-pack pineapple, not drained
2 c. buttermilk
8 oz. Cool Whip® whipped topping, thawed

Mix Jell-O® and pineapple in saucepan and bring to boil. Let cool. Add buttermilk and mix well. Refrigerate and let thicken. Fold in Cool Whip® with mixer and chill overnight.

Nutrition facts per serving: 144 calories; 2.7 g protein; 3.5 g fat; 24.0 g carbohydrates; 0 g fiber; 85 mg sodium. 12 servings.

An old family recipe that came from my mother.
Judy Fishel Joyce, member Forsyth County Public Library Board of Trustees

Pistachio Dessert

1 pkg. Jell-O® pistachio flavor instant pudding and pie filling mix
15.5-oz. can crushed juice-pack pineapple, not drained
1 c. miniature marshmallows
½ c. chopped pecans or black walnuts
8 oz. Cool Whip® whipped topping, thawed

Combine pudding mix and pineapple. Blend in marshmallows and nuts. Fold in Cool Whip®. Chill and serve.

Nutrition facts per serving: 299 calories; 1.1 g protein; 12.8 g fat; 42.0 g carbohydrates; 0.9 g fiber; 239 mg sodium. 6 servings.

Wanda Wadkins, former staff

Strawberry Cream

1 pkg. strawberry flavor gelatin
½ c. boiling water
1½ c. fresh strawberries
3 c. whipping cream, divided
1 tsp. vanilla extract
1 Tbsp. granulated sugar

Pour boiling water over gelatin, stir to dissolve and let stand 5 minutes to soften. Meanwhile, put strawberries in blender with just enough cream to cover and blend. Drizzle softened gelatin into blender and process until smooth. In separate bowl, whip remaining cream with vanilla and sugar until stiff, then fold into strawberry mixture. Pour into 4-cup mold and chill.

Nutrition facts per serving: 372 calories; 3.1 g protein; 33.2 g fat; 17.9 g carbohydrates; 0.7 g fiber; 66 mg sodium. 8 servings.

Ann Gehlen, in whose memory the Forsyth County Public Library Employee of the Year Award is named.

Sweet Pecans

2½ c. (1 lb.) pecan halves
2 Tbsp. granulated sugar
1 Tbsp. ground cinnamon
1¼ tsp. salt
3 Tbsp. butter, melted

Preheat oven to 350ºF. Mix all ingredients except butter in bowl. Add melted butter and mix well. Transfer to shallow pan and bake 25 to 30 minutes, stirring occasionally.

Nutrition facts per serving: 229 calories; 2.5 g protein; 23.1 g fat; 6.8 g carbohydrates; 3.0 g fiber; 326 mg sodium. 10 servings.

Served at On The Same Page program featuring To Kill a Mockingbird *by Harper Lee.*
Merrikay Brown, current staff

Haystacks

2 c. butterscotch chips
8 oz. peanuts
5-oz. can chow mein noodles

Melt butterscotch chips in saucepan over low heat, stirring constantly. Stir in peanuts and noodles. Drop by spoonfuls onto waxed paper. Let stand until firm.

Nutrition facts per serving: 169 calories; 3.2 g protein; 11.3 g fat; 15.3 g carbohydrates; 1.2 g fiber; 96 mg sodium. 24 servings.

From my mother, Rosalie Luck
Lara Luck, current staff

Bourbon Fudge

1 oz. slivered almonds or broken pecans
2 c. semi-sweet chocolate chips
(I always use Nestlé®)
14-oz. can sweetened condensed milk
¼ c. Maker's Mark® bourbon
½ tsp. orange extract

Toast nuts and cool, then sprinkle evenly in greased 8"x8" pan. Combine chocolate chips and milk in large bowl and cook in microwave 2 minutes on high. Remove from microwave and stir until smooth. Add bourbon and orange extract and mix well. Pour mixture into prepared pan and chill well. Turn out with nuts on top and cut into small pieces.

Nutrition facts per piece: 87 calories; 1.3 g protein; 4.2 g fat; 11.5 g carbohydrates; 0.7 g fiber; 14 mg sodium. 36 pieces.

A holiday favorite! Will produce giddiness with a relatively small amount of alcohol.
Julie James, former staff

"Sweet food of sweetly uttered knowledge."

Sir Philip Sidney, 1554-1586
The Defense of Poesy

BEVERAGES

Cheerwine® Punch

2 ltr. Cheerwine® cherry soda
1 ltr. ginger ale
2 46-oz. cans pineapple juice

Mix all ingredients in large punch bowl and serve over ice.

Nutrition facts per serving: 56 calories; 0.2 g protein; 0 g fat; 14.3 g carbohydrates; 0 g fiber; 5 mg sodium. 50 servings (4-oz.).

Jackie Jones, current staff

Cinnamon Punch

1 c. water
½ c. granulated sugar
½ c. red cinnamon candies
4 ltr. chilled ginger ale
46-oz. bottle apple cider

Combine water, sugar and cinnamon candies in small saucepan and bring to boil. Reduce heat and simmer uncovered for 3 minutes or until candies melt, stirring constantly. Cool completely. Just before serving, combine cooled cinnamon syrup, ginger ale and apple cider in large punch bowl.

Nutrition facts per serving: 94 calories; 0 g protein; 0 g fat; 23.8 g carbohydrates; 0 g fiber; 11 mg sodium. 30 servings (6-oz.).

DeLois Cue, current staff

Citrus Mint Tea Cooler

1 c. boiling water
3 regular tea bags
2 Tbsp. chopped fresh mint
2/3 c. granulated sugar
2/3 c. fresh grapefruit juice
2/3 c. fresh lemon juice
2 c. cold water

Pour boiling water over tea bags and mint, cover and let steep for 5 minutes. Pour mixture through wire mesh strainer, discarding tea bags and mint. Stir in sugar, juices and cold water. Serve over ice. Note: For an attractive presentation, freeze small mint leaves in the ice cubes.

Nutrition facts per serving: 154 calories; 0.2 g protein; 0 g fat; 39.9 g carbohydrates; 0.4 g fiber; 1 mg sodium. 4 servings.

Served at Cooking With Herbs program, part of "Successful Gardening at the Library" series.
Janelle Kent, Extension Agent, NC Cooperative Extension Service

Lime Freeze Punch

2 pkgs. lemon lime flavor Kool-Aid® drink mix
2 c. granulated sugar (or to taste)
1 gal. cold water
2 ltr. ginger ale
46-oz. can pineapple juice
crushed ice

Combine all ingredients in large punch bowl and serve.

Alternate method: Mix Kool-Aid®, sugar and water and freeze in gallon jug. An hour before serving, remove jug from freezer to soften. Cut the jug to remove frozen mixture. Combine frozen mixture and pineapple juice in large punch bowl just before serving. Do not add crushed ice or ginger ale.

Nutrition facts per serving: 95 calories; 0.2 g protein; 0 g fat; 24.4 g carbohydrates; 0 g fiber; 8 mg sodium. 32 servings.

Mary Dula, current staff

"Is there no Latin word for tea? Upon my soul, if I had known that I would have let the vulgar stuff alone."

Hilaire Belloc, 1879-1953
On Nothing, On Tea

Jennifer Huffingham's Russian Tea Mix

1¼ c. instant orange flavor breakfast drink mix (such as Tang®)
2/3 c. instant iced tea mix with sugar and lemon
1 tsp. ground cloves
1 tsp. ground cinnamon
1 tsp. ground allspice
¼ tsp. grated lemon rind
¼ tsp. grated orange rind

Combine all ingredients. Stir well. Store mix in airtight container. To serve, place 3 to 4 tsp. mix in cup. Add 1 cup boiling water and stir well.

Nutrition facts per serving: 58 calories; 0 g protein; 0 g fat; 15.6 g carbohydrates; 0.1 g fiber; 1 mg sodium. 24 servings.

Jennifer Huffingham was my best friend in Library School at FSU. She is a part-time reference librarian in the Jacksonville Public Library system in Jacksonville, Florida.
Elizabeth Skinner, current staff

Al Sooman's Christmas Punch

1½ c. granulated sugar
1 qt. orange juice
½ c. lemon juice
1 qt. cold strong tea
15.5-oz. can sliced pineapple in heavy syrup, not drained
10-oz. jar maraschino cherries, not drained
2 lemons, shredded
1 fifth (25.4 oz.) bourbon
1 fifth (25.4 oz.) peach brandy (may substitute apple or apricot brandy)
2 trays ice cubes
2 bottles (25.4 oz. each) champagne

Dissolve sugar in fruit juices and tea. Add all remaining ingredients except ice and champagne. Mix well and refrigerate at least 1 hour. Just before serving, add ice and champagne. Stir gently.

Nutrition facts per serving: 132 calories; 0.2 g protein; 0 g fat; 15.5 g carbohydrates; 0.4 g fiber; 2 mg sodium. 60 servings (4-oz.).

Bill Roberts, former Director, Forsyth County Public Library
Editor's note: This was a much-anticipated staple of Library Association get-togethers for 30 years!

Close to 'South by Southwest' Cactus Nectar Margarita

lime wedge
coarse salt (sold in plastic dipping containers)
ice cubes
1 oz. tequila (Sauza Gold® recommended)
1 oz. mezcal (note: the mezcal makes it "smokier;" if you like it, use more with less gold tequila)
½ oz. triple sec, Grand Marnier®, or Gran Gala®, or a combination of liqueurs
good splash of orange juice (Tropicana® with mandarin orange juice recommended)
1½ oz. lime juice

Rub rim of old fashioned glass with lime wedge. Dip in salt to coat. Add ice cubes. In separate "shaker" (I use Tupperware® container with pour lid) with some ice cubes in it, combine tequila, mezcal, liqueur, orange juice and lime juice. Shake it up. Pour into glass. Garnish with lime wedge. Do not drive!

Alternate slightly less powerful version: Substitute 2 jiggers of Franco's Lime® bar mix (decent ingredients, but cool—it's very green) and some lime juice for the 1½ oz. lime juice.

Nutrition facts per serving: 239 calories; 0.7 g protein; 0 g fat; 19.1 g carbohydrates; 0.5 g fiber; 588 mg sodium. 1 serving.

This is close to the recipe at South by Southwest, a local restaurant, which Mary McAfee and I enjoy and which they no longer have on the menu but will gladly fix.
Dave Fergusson, current staff

> "i brood on beer
> my scampering whiffle snoot
> on beer says he"
>
> Don Marquis, 1878-1937
> *archy and mehitabel*

Peach Mimosas

- 5 c. peach nectar, chilled
- 2 c. champagne, chilled
- 1 c. cranberry juice cocktail, chilled

Combine all ingredients in punch bowl and serve immediately. For Virgin Peach Mimosas, substitute ginger ale for champagne.

Nutrition facts per serving: 75 calories; 0.3 g protein; 0 g fat; 14.1 g carbohydrates; 0.3 g fiber; 7 mg sodium. 16 servings.

Adapted from a beverage served at a bachelorette party. A smooth alternative for those who don't care for the acidity of orange mimosas.
Jenny Barrett, current staff

Colombian Sangria

- 1 apple, cored and thinly sliced
- 1 orange, sliced crosswise
- ½ c. brandy
- ½ c. Grand Marnier®
- 1 bottle dry red wine (I like Chilean Cabernet Sauvignon)

Soak apple and orange in brandy and Grand Marnier® all day or overnight. Add red wine 20-30 minutes before serving.

Nutrition facts per serving: 222 calories; 0.1 g protein; 0 g fat; 19.6 g carbohydrates; 0.9 g fiber; 4 mg sodium. 8 servings.

I have a staff member who lived in Colombia and she gave me this. We love it!
Julie Walker, former staff and current PINES Program Director, Georgia Public Library Service

Hot Scotch

2 oz. butterscotch schnapps
1 pkg. instant cocoa
whipped cream (optional)

Prepare cocoa according to package directions. Stir in schnapps. Garnish with whipped cream if desired.

Nutrition facts per serving(without whipped cream): 312 calories; 1.0 g protein; 1.0 g fat; 38.0 g carbohydrates; 1.0 g fiber; 102 mg sodium.
1 serving.

Teresa Floyd, current staff

"The divine drink, which builds up resistance and fights fatigue. A cup of this precious drink [cocoa] permits a man to walk for a whole day without food."

Montezuma II, 1466-1520

BREAKFAST

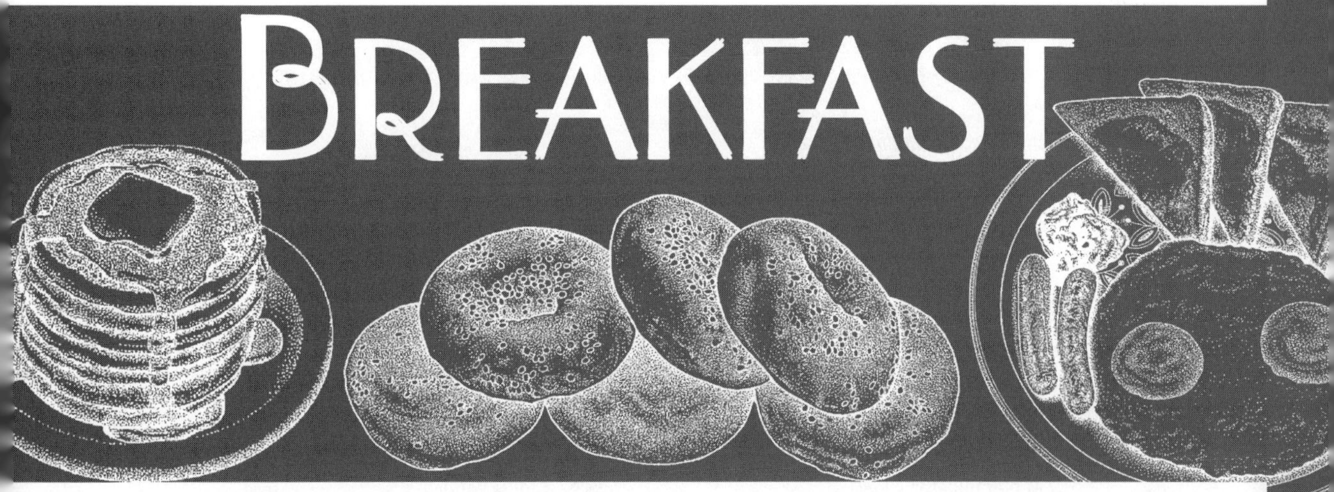

Always Perfect Banana Bread

1 stick (½ c.) margarine, softened
1 c. granulated sugar
2 eggs
1½ c. all-purpose flour
1 tsp. baking soda
¼ tsp. salt
3 ripe bananas, mashed
½ c. chopped nuts (I prefer pecans)

Preheat oven to 350ºF. Cream margarine with sugar. Add eggs and beat. Add flour, baking soda and salt and mix well. Fold in bananas and nuts. Bake in greased loaf pan for 1 hour.

Nutrition facts per serving: 156 calories; 2.0 g protein; 7.2 g fat; 21.9 g carbohydrates; 0.9 g fiber; 152 mg sodium. 20 servings.

Elizabeth Skinner, current staff

Banana Bread

2 c. all-purpose flour
¾ c. granulated sugar
¾ tsp. baking soda
½ tsp. salt
1¼ c. toasted walnuts, coarsely chopped
3 very ripe soft bananas, mashed (1½ c.)
3 oz. vanilla yogurt
2 eggs, lightly beaten
¾ stick (6 Tbsp.) butter, melted and cooled
2 tsp. vanilla extract

Adjust oven rack to lower-middle position and preheat to 350ºF. Whisk flour, sugar, baking soda, salt and walnuts together in large bowl and set aside. Mix mashed bananas, yogurt, eggs, butter and vanilla with wooden spoon in medium bowl. Lightly fold banana mixture into dry ingredients until just combined and batter looks thick and chunky. Scrape batter into greased and floured loaf pan. Bake until loaf is golden brown and toothpick inserted in center comes out clean, about 55 minutes. Cool in pan for 5 minutes, then transfer to wire rack. Serve warm or at room temperature.

Nutrition facts per serving: 186 calories; 3.1 g protein; 9.4 g fat; 23.8 g carbohydrates; 1.1 g fiber; 149 mg sodium. 20 servings.

When you have a few bananas you don't want to throw out, this is a great, quick, and easy recipe. It also makes great muffins, with or without the walnuts.
Mackenzie Krell. "We love the resources that the library offers and our children love to pick out their own books and videos each week and for nighttime stories. They enjoy picking out which one we are going to read first. It helps their little imaginations in so many ways."

Banana Muffins

4 med. overripe bananas
¾ c. granulated sugar
1 egg, slightly beaten
⅔ stick (⅓ c.) butter, melted
1½ c. all-purpose flour
1 tsp. baking powder
1 tsp. baking soda
pinch salt

Preheat oven to 300°F. Mash bananas and add sugar and egg. Mix in butter, then add remaining ingredients and mix well. Pour into greased or lined muffin tins. Bake 20 minutes.

Nutrition facts per serving: 193 calories; 2.5 g protein; 6.0 g fat; 33.9 g carbohydrates; 1.3 g fiber; 227 mg sodium. 12 muffins.

This is from South Africa where friends "pop in" for tea. Quick and easy to make. Best for really overripe bananas. Barbara Hill, Friend of the Library. "Arriving in USA from SA with no friends here, the library (in Philly) was my first 'friend.'"

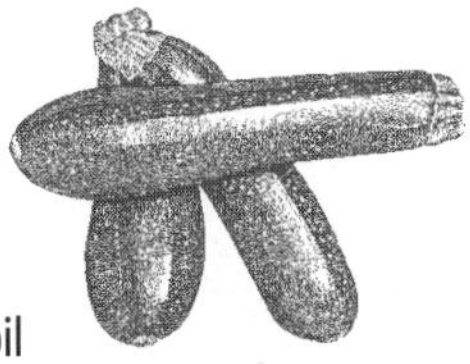

Zucchini Bread

2 c. all-purpose flour
2 tsp. baking soda
2 tsp. ground cinnamon
¼ tsp. ground allspice
½ tsp. salt
1 c. granulated sugar
3 eggs
¾ c. vegetable oil
¼ c. water
2 c. shredded zucchini, squeezed in tea towel to remove excess moisture
½ c. raisins
½ c. chopped nuts

Preheat oven to 350°F. Combine first 6 ingredients in large bowl. Add eggs, oil, and water and mix well. Stir in zucchini, raisins, and nuts. Pour into 1 large or 2 small greased and floured loaf pans. Bake for 1 to 1½ hours or until toothpick stuck in center comes out clean.

Nutrition facts per serving: 201 calories; 3.0 g protein; 11.0 g fat; 23.6 g carbohydrates; 0.9 g fiber; 196 mg sodium. 16 servings.

Kathleen Wheeless, current staff

"The critical period in matrimony is breakfast-time."

Sir Alan Patrick Herbert, 1890-1971
Uncommon Law

Easy Scones

4 c. all-purpose flour
1 tsp. baking soda
¾ stick (6 Tbsp.) butter, melted
1 c. granulated sugar
1½ c. Craisins® dried cranberries or raisins
2 c. buttermilk
1 Tbsp. vanilla extract
extra sugar for sprinkling on top

Preheat oven to 425°F. Mix flour and baking soda in large bowl. Add melted butter and mix well. Add sugar and Craisins® and mix again. Add buttermilk and vanilla and knead lightly. Flour hands and make golf-ball-sized clumps. Place on greased baking sheet. Sprinkle lightly with sugar. Bake for 15 to 20 minutes or until they begin to brown. Remove from oven and cool. Note: You can add chopped nuts along with Craisins® for different consistency.

Nutrition facts per serving: 257 calories; 4.3 g protein; 4.8 g fat; 48.9 g carbohydrates; 1.7 g fiber; 156 mg sodium. 16 scones.

These are great for breakfast with homemade preserves.
Dr. Tom Shown, Friend of Southside Library. "The library is a great place to learn and expand your horizons. Andrew Carnegie was such an inspirational benefactor."

Orange-Scented Scones

1¾ c. all-purpose flour
2 tsp. baking powder
½ tsp. kosher salt
1 Tbsp. granulated sugar
grated zest of 1 med. orange
1 stick (½ c.) unsalted butter, cut into 1/3" cubes
¾ c. buttermilk, divided
2 Tbsp. turbinado sugar or raw sugar

Preheat oven to 400°F. Combine flour, baking powder, salt, and sugar in mixer. Mix in orange zest. Add butter and mix just until coated with flour. Butter chunks should remain fairly large—no less than half their original size. With mixer set on slow speed, add 2/3 cup buttermilk and mix until just absorbed. Stop mixing when dough begins to pull away from sides of bowl. Scrape dough from bowl and shape it into ball. With well-floured fingers, pat dough into 7" diameter disk. Cut disk into eighths. Set scones on baking sheet lined with kitchen parchment and brush tops with remaining buttermilk. Sprinkle with turbinado sugar and bake until well browned, about 15 to 20 minutes.

Nutrition facts per serving: 230 calories; 3.7 g protein; 11.9 g fat; 26.8 g carbohydrates; 0.8 g fiber; 295 mg sodium. 8 scones.

Ben Morgan, current staff

Orange Scones

3 c. all-purpose flour
½ tsp. baking soda
¾ c. granulated sugar
2 tsp. grated orange rind
1 stick (½ c.) unsalted butter
¾ c. buttermilk
¾ c. currants or chopped pecans

Preheat oven to 400°F. Combine dry ingredients. Mix in orange rind. Cut in butter. Add buttermilk and mix until just absorbed. Knead in currants or pecans. Knead dough just enough to moisten. Too much kneading will make scones tough. Pat dough flat and cut into 12 pieces. Set scones on baking sheet. Bake 10 to 12 minutes.

Nutrition facts per serving (made with currants): 262 calories; 4.2 g protein; 8.0 g fat; 43.7 g carbohydrates; 1.4 g fiber; 148 mg sodium.
Per serving (made with pecans): 283 calories; 4.5 g protein; 12.9 g fat; 38.0 g carbohydrates; 1.5 g fiber; 147 mg sodium.
12 scones.

Susan Peterson, former staff

Blueberry Buckle

¾ c. granulated sugar
¼ c. shortening or margarine
1 egg
½ c. milk
2 c. all-purpose flour
2 tsp. baking powder
2 tsp. salt
2 c. frozen blueberries

Topping

½ c. granulated sugar
⅓ c. all-purpose flour
1 tsp. ground cinnamon
¼ c. cold butter or margarine

Preheat oven to 350°F. To prepare batter, mix sugar and shortening thoroughly. Stir in egg and milk. Mix flour, baking powder and salt and add to sugar mixture. Gently add blueberries. Pour into lightly greased 8″x8″ pan. In separate bowl, prepare topping by cutting all ingredients together until crumbly, not smooth. Crumble topping over batter and bake for 50 minutes or until top crust is browned. Note: This recipe can be converted to vegan by replacing egg with 3 Tbsp. egg substitute and milk with soy milk.

Nutrition facts per serving: 357 calories; 4.8 g protein; 12.3 g fat; 58.0 g carbohydrates; 1.8 g fiber; 694 mg sodium. 9 servings.

Former staff member Julie James would often bring in this coffee cake, warm from the oven, to get the Business & Science staff going in the morning. Julie got this recipe from Marcia Frutuozo, a staff member at Thomasville Public Library.
Kathleen Wheeless, current staff

Moravian Sugar Cake

2 pkgs. active dry yeast
½ c. granulated sugar
½ c. warm water (110ºF)
¾ c. water
2 Tbsp. non-fat powdered milk
¼ c. instant mashed potato flakes
½ tsp. salt
2 sticks (1 c.) butter, melted and cooled, divided
2 eggs
3 c. all-purpose flour
1 c. packed brown sugar
1 tsp. ground cinnamon

In large bowl, sprinkle yeast and ½ tsp. of sugar onto warm water. Let set until yeast bubbles and mixture is foamy, about 5 to 10 minutes. Add remaining water, powdered milk, potato flakes, salt, ½ cup melted butter, eggs and 1 cup flour. Beat with wooden spoon. Add remaining flour (or a little more if needed) to reach consistency of soft bread dough. Place in greased bowl and turn to grease top. Let rise until double in size, about 1 hour. Punch down dough and pat into greased 12″x17″ pan (rimmed cookie sheet will work). Let rise 30 minutes.

Preheat oven to 375ºF. Sprinkle dough with brown sugar and cinnamon. Using your fingers, poke indentations all over dough. Drizzle remaining ½ cup of melted butter over top. Bake for 12 to 15 minutes or until golden brown. May be served warm or at room temperature.

Nutrition facts per serving: 186 calories; 2.6 g protein; 8.2 g fat; 26.0 g carbohydrates; 0.6 g fiber; 139 mg sodium. 24 servings.

Adapted from North Carolina and Old Salem Cookery *by Beth Tartan.*
Nancy Metzgar, current staff

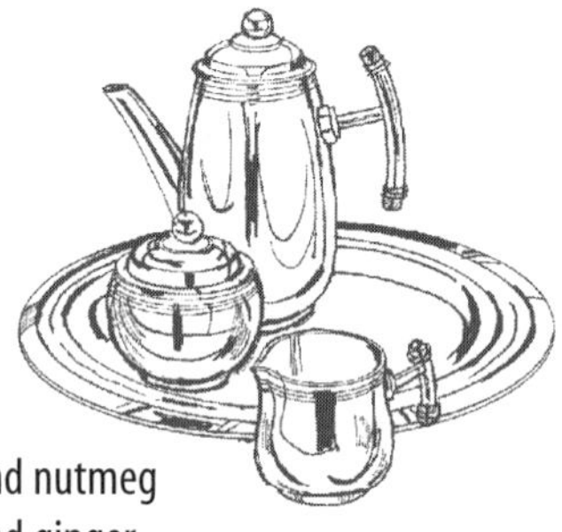

Quick Coffee Cake

1 c. unsifted all-purpose flour
1 c. unsifted whole wheat flour
¾ c. old-fashioned rolled oats
1/3 c. firmly packed light brown sugar
1 Tbsp. baking powder
2 tsp. ground cinnamon
½ tsp. ground nutmeg
¼ tsp. ground ginger
pinch of salt
1 stick (½ c.) margarine
1 c. unsweetened apple juice

Preheat oven to 350ºF. Grease and flour 9″x9″ baking pan. In large bowl, combine flours, ½ cup of oats, sugar, baking powder, cinnamon, nutmeg, ginger, and salt. Remove ½ cup of mixture to small bowl and add remaining ¼ cup oats to that bowl. Cut 2 Tbsp. of margarine into mixture in small bowl and set aside. Cut remaining margarine into flour mixture in large bowl. Stir in apple juice until well combined. Pour batter into prepared pan. Top with reserved oat mixture from small bowl. Bake about 40 minutes or until knife inserted in center comes out clean. Let cake cool to room temperature.

Nutrition facts per serving: 274 calories; 4.3 g protein; 12.0 g fat; 38.2 g carbohydrates; 2.9 g fiber; 140 mg sodium. 8 servings.

Ben Morgan, current staff

Breakfast Smoothie

1 c. nonfat plain or vanilla yogurt
$1\frac{1}{3}$ c. frozen strawberries, no sugar added
1 kiwi, peeled and quartered
1 ripe banana, peeled and quartered

Place all ingredients into blender and process on pulse until mixture is milkshake consistency.

Nutrition facts per serving: 320 calories; 12.3 g protein; 2.3 g fat; 7.2 g carbohydrates; 9.9 g fiber; 140 mg sodium. 1 serving.

Jessica Cole, current staff

Breakfast Casserole

4 slices bread
1 lb. loose pork sausage
1 c. sharp cheddar cheese, grated
6 eggs
2 c. milk
1 tsp. dry mustard (optional)
1 tsp. salt
dash of pepper

Preheat oven to 350ºF. Tear bread into pieces and arrange in greased 9"x13" baking dish. Brown sausage and drain. Spoon sausage over bread. Sprinkle with cheese. Beat together remaining ingredients and pour over bread and sausage. Bake for 35 to 40 minutes. Cheese will rise to top during baking. Note: This can be refrigerated overnight and baked for breakfast the next morning.

Nutrition facts per serving: 421 calories; 25.5 g protein; 28.0 g fat; 13.7 g carbohydrates; 0.7 g fiber; 1102 mg sodium. 6 servings.

Betsy Hensley, current staff

Cheddarliscious Egg and Sausage Casserole

2 lb. loose pork sausage
1 loaf (16-20 slices) bread
8 oz. sharp cheddar cheese, shredded
12 eggs
2 c. milk
1 c. sliced mushrooms
1 c. diced onion
1 c. chopped green bell pepper
3 Tbsp. Worcestershire sauce
crushed red pepper to taste (optional)

Brown sausage in skillet, drain excess fat, and set aside. Trim crusts from bread and layer half of loaf in bottom of large buttered casserole. Add layer of crumbled browned sausage and layer of cheese. Stir together eggs, milk, mushrooms, onion, bell pepper, Worcestershire sauce and crushed red pepper (if desired). Stir until blended and pour into casserole. Place remaining bread on top, cover and refrigerate overnight. Next morning, preheat oven to 350ºF and bake for 30 minutes. Remove from oven and let set for 10 minutes before serving. Note: You can combine browned sausage and cheese with egg mixture instead of making layers if you prefer.

Nutrition facts per serving: 472 calories; 26.4 g protein; 27.3 g fat; 27.5 g carbohydrates; 2.2 g fiber; 908 mg sodium. 12 servings.

Arneita Hairston, current staff

Sausage Cheese Muffins

1 pkg. (6) English muffins
1 lb. loose pork sausage
15-oz. jar Cheez Whiz® processed cheese spread

Toast English muffins and set aside. Brown sausage and drain off excess fat. Add Cheez Whiz® to sausage and stir until melted. Spread sausage/cheese mixture on muffins and serve warm. Note: Can be frozen and reheated in microwave.

Nutrition facts per serving: 259 calories; 10.8 g protein; 15.3 g fat; 17.7 g carbohydrates; 0.8 g fiber; 929 mg sodium. 12 servings.

Teresa Floyd, current staff

"Over buttered scones and crumpets
Weeping, weeping multitudes
Droop in a hundred A.B.C.'s"

Thomas Stearns Eliot, 1888-1965
A Cooking Egg

Quiche Formula

1 unbaked pie shell (I use Pillsbury® refrigerated)
¼ lb. cheese, any variety you like, grated
2 to 3 c. (approx.) spinach, mushrooms, asparagus, broccoli, tomatoes, artichokes, or anything you like
fresh herbs to taste, anything you like
3 eggs, or the equivalent in Egg Beaters® egg substitute
1 c. milk

Preheat oven to 375ºF. Prick pie crust with fork and par-bake 6 to 8 minutes or until very lightly browned. Remove from oven and spread half of cheese over crust to melt. This protects crust from getting too soggy. Put vegetables and herbs in crust, then whisk together eggs and milk and pour over vegetables. Bake 35 to 40 minutes or until mostly firm. Remove from oven and spread rest of cheese over top to melt. Let stand 10 minutes before slicing. Serve warm or cold.

Nutrition facts per serving: 310 calories; 10.3 g protein; 19.2 g fat; 21.8 g carbohydrates; 1.3 g fiber; 317 mg sodium. 6 servings.

Adapted from The Enchanted Broccoli Forest *by Mollie Katzen.*
Julie James, former staff

"Sometimes it's a good day to die, and sometimes it's a good day to have breakfast."

Sherman Alexie, 1966–
Smoke Signals

AKNOWLEDGMENTS

Centennial Cookbook Committee

William Durham, Chairman
Betty Allegrone
Jenny Barrett
Yolanda Bolden
Vince Cannino
Allison Carmola
DeLois Cue
Esmirna Esparza
Erica Fields
Teresa Floyd
Julie James
Jackie Jones
Lise Keppler
Mary McAfee
Anne McLeod
Rob Norwood
Melinda Pennington
Carolyn Price
Decca Riedel
Helene Robinson
Jacque Smith
Sylvia Thompson

Library Administration

Sylvia Sprinkle-Hamlin, Director of Libraries
Dave Fergusson, Deputy Director
Mary McAfee, Assistant Director

Board of Trustees

Donna L. Staley, Chairman
Thomas F. Looby, Vice Chairman
Beaufort O. Bailey
Diane M. Greer
Judy F. Joyce
Kathleen A. Sides
Juanita Anthony Tatum

Special Contributions

Lise Keppler
Rob Norwood
Bob Shar
John Via

INDEX

24-Hour Salad,17
7-Up® Pound Cake, 83

abbreviations, xv
Advent Bread, 72
African Chicken and Rice, 26
Al Sooman's Christmas Punch, 122
Always Perfect Banana Bread, 126
Ambrosia, 20
Apple Pie, 94
Apple Pound Cake, 78
apples
  Apple Pie, 94
  Apple Pound Cake, 78
  Big Mama's Apple Cake, 78
  Fresh Apple Cake, 79
Armenian Lentil Soup, 53
Asian Salmon, 39
Asparagus Rolls, 9
Athens Greek Couscous, 66

Baked Fruit Compote, 67
Baked Onion Dip, 2
Banana Bread, 126
Banana Muffins, 127
Banana Oatmeal Cookies, 102
Banana Pudding, 110
bananas
  Always Perfect Banana Bread, 126
  Ambrosia, 20
  Banana Bread, 126
  Banana Muffins, 127
  Banana Oatmeal Cookies, 102
  Banana Pudding, 110
  Jessica's Fruit Salad, 21
  Orange Fruit Salad, 22
Barbecued Chicken, 27
Barrett Family Macaroni and Cheese, 42
Barrett Family Spaghetti and Meatballs, 37
Basic Vinaigrette, 15
beans
  Armenian Lentil Soup, 53
  Black Bean Hummus, 2
  Black Bean Salsa, 23
  Broad Bean Salad, 12
  Calico Salad, 12
  Cheesy Mushroom Green Bean Casserole, 60
  Green Bean Casserole, 59
  Herbed Lentils and Rice, 44
  Ranch Style Baked Beans, 65
  Roasted Beans with Garlic and Olives, 46
  Spicy Chili, 50
  Vegetable Casserole, 60
  Vegetarian Chili, Cincinnati-Style, 51
beef
  Barrett Family Spaghetti and Meatballs, 37
  Best Ever Crock-Pot® Stew, 48
  Brunswick Stew, 49
  Carmola Quick Spaghetti, 36
  Chopped South Carolina Barbecue, 33
  Decca's Combined Family Meatloaf, 35
  Five-Hour Stew, 49
  Homemade Vegetable Beef Soup, 53
  Jennifer's Meatloaf, 35
  Johnny Brazili, 38
  Plantation Casserole, 34
  Ranch Style Baked Beans, 65
  Spicy Chili, 50
  Sweet and Sour Meatballs, 36
Best Coconut Cake, 79
Best Ever Crock-Pot® Stew, 48
Big Mama's Apple Cake, 78
Big Mama's Lemon Pound Cake, 81
Black Bean Hummus, 2
Black Bean Salsa, 23
Blue Cheese Ball, 6
Blueberry Buckle, 129
Bob Rickert's Shrimp Cocktail Sauce, 10
Bonnie's Clam Dip, 2
Bourbon Fudge, 118
Breakfast Casserole, 131
Breakfast Smoothie, 131
Broad Bean Salad (Fool Midammis), 12
Broccoli Casserole, 58
Broccoli Cheese Casserole, 58
Broccoli Corn Bread, 70
Broccoli Rice Casserole, 59
Brunswick Stew, 49

Burgundy Bacon Vinaigrette, 24
Butterscotch Brownies, 106

Calico Salad, 12
candies
  Bourbon Fudge, 118
  Haystacks, 118
Carmola Quick Spaghetti, 36
casseroles
  Barrett Family Macaroni and Cheese, 42
  Breakfast Casserole, 131
  Broccoli Casserole, 58
  Broccoli Cheese Casserole, 58
  Broccoli Rice Casserole, 59
  Cheddarliscious Egg and Sausage Casserole, 131
  Cheesy Mushroom Green Bean Casserole, 60
  Down Home Ham and Potato Casserole, 34
  Emily Williams's Swiss Chicken Casserole, 28
  Garlic Cheese Grits, 66
  Gratin of Root Vegetables, 64
  Green Bean Casserole, 59
  Herbed Lentils and Rice, 44
  Homestyle Four-Cheese Macaroni, 42
  Mushroom Rice, 65
  Pineapple Casserole, 68
  Plantation Casserole, 34
  Ranch Style Baked Beans, 65
  Seven Seas Casserole, 41
  Squash Casserole, 61
  Squash and Cheese Casserole, 61
  Sweet Potato Casserole, 62
  Texas Chicken Loaf, 30
  Vegetable Casserole, 60
Cheddarliscious Egg and Sausage Casserole, 131
Cheerwine® Punch, 120
Cheese Krispies, 7
Cheese Pennies, 8
cheesecake
  Cream Cheese Cake, 92
  Robert's Ginger Cheesecake, 92
Cheesy Mushroom Green Bean Casserole, 60
Cherry Frosting, 83
Cherry Pound Cake, 82
chicken
  African Chicken and Rice, 26
  Barbecued Chicken, 27
  Brunswick Stew, 49
  Chicken Crescents, 30
  Chicken Stew, 50
  Citrus Grilled Chicken, 27
  Emily Williams's Swiss Chicken Casserole, 28
  Healthy Chicken Salad, 31
  Hot Chicken Salad, 32
  Jazzed Up Chicken, 29
  Karen's Mexican Chicken, 29
  Lemon Blueberry Chicken Salad, 31
  Miss Annie's Baked Chicken and Gravy, 28
  Mom's Chicken Noodle Soup, 52
  Plantation Casserole, 34
  Texas Chicken Loaf, 30
Chicken Crescents, 30
Chicken Stew, 50
Chocolate Chess Pie, 100
Chocolate on Chocolate Cake, 84
Chopped South Carolina Barbecue, 33
Cinnamon Punch, 120
Citrus Grilled Chicken, 27
Citrus Mint Tea Cooler, 120
Close to 'South by Southwest' Cactus Nectar Margarita, 122
cocktail sauce
  Bob Rickert's Shrimp Cocktail Sauce, 10
coffee cakes
  Blueberry Buckle, 129
  Moravian Sugar Cake, 130
  Quick Coffee Cake, 130
  Sock-It-To-Me Cake, 88
Colombian Sangria, 123
Cool Rise Bread, 73
Copper Pennies, 14
couscous
  Athens Greek Couscous, 66
Crabbies, 8
cranberries
  Cranberry Relish, 68

Jazzed Up Chicken, 20
Joyce's Cranberry Salad, 20
Cranberry Relish, 68
Cream Cheese Cake, 92
Cream Cheese Frosting, 87
Curried Pea Soup, 54

Decca's Combined Family Meatloaf, 35
Dena Southard's Ginger Snaps, 105
Dip for Tortilla Chips, 4
Down Home Ham and Potato Casserole, 34

Eastern Carolina Barbecue, the Cheater's Version, 33
Easy Mexican Dip, 4
Easy Rice Pudding 'Comfort Food', 110
Easy Scones, 128
Eggplant Supper Soup, 52
Emily Williams' s Swiss Chicken Casserole, 28

Fennel Seed Vinaigrette, 23
Five-Hour Stew, 49
Fool Midammis *see* Broad Bean Salad
French Cherry Pie, 94
French Dressing, 14
French Vanilla Ice Cream, 113
Fresh Apple Cake, 79
frostings
Cherry, 83
Cream Cheese, 87
Lemon, 82
Rich and Creamy Chocolate, 85
Seven-Minute, 81
Frozen Lemonade Pie, 95
Fruit and Angel Dessert, 114

Garlic Cheese Grits, 66
Garlic Rosemary Potatoes, 63
Georgia Shrimp Bake, 40
gingerbread
Southern Gingerbread and Lemon Sauce, 90
Grandmother Wheeless's Pumpkin Pie, 98
Granny Rolls, 74
Granny's Cherry Yum-Yum, 115
Gratin of Root Vegetables, 64
Green Bean Casserole, 59
guacamole
Julie's Guacamole, 3

Haystacks, 118
Healthy Chicken Salad, 31
Herbed Lentils and Rice, 44
Homemade Vegetable Beef Soup, 53
Homestyle Four-Cheese Macaroni, 42
Hot Chicken Salad, 32
Hot Scotch, 124

Ice Box Rolls, 74
ice cream
French Vanilla, 113
Mother's Ice Cream Crunch, 114
Indian Boiled Cookies, 103
Italian Cream Cake, 87

jambalaya
Shrimp Jambalaya, 39
Jazzed Up Chicken, 29
Jell-O® Salad, 19
Jennifer Huffingham's Russian Tea Mix, 121
Jennifer's Favorite Pumpkin Pie, 96
Jennifer's Meatloaf, 35
Jessica's Fruit Salad, 21
Johnny Brazili, 38
Joy White's Spinach Spread, 5
Joyce's Cranberry Salad, 20
Julie's Guacamole, 3

Karen's Mexican Chicken, 29

Lane Cake, 86
lasagna
Robert's Lasagna, 38
Layered Taco Dip, 4
Lemon Bars, 108
Lemon Blueberry Chicken Salad, 31
Lemon Frosting, 82
Lime Freeze Punch, 121
Low-Fat Potato Salad, 17

Marcia Bernsten's English Toffee Cookies, 105
margaritas
Close to 'South by Southwest' Cactus Nectar Margarita, 122

Margot Wharton's Tex-Mex Dip, 5
Marinated Cabbage Slaw, 13
Marinated Cucumber Salad, 13
Marinated Tomatoes, 14
Million Dollar Pie, 96
Miss Annie's Baked Chicken and Gravy, 28
Mocha Charlottes, 111
Mom's Chicken Noodle Soup, 52
Mom's Whole Wheat Bread, 76
Moravian Sugar Cake, 130
Mother Blount's Fantastic Ambrosia, 21
Mother's Ice Cream Crunch, 114
Mr. Roberts' Punch *see* Al Sooman's Christmas Punch
Mrs. Williams's Pumpkin Pie, 97
Mushroom Rice, 65

Noodles and Broccoli with Saffron, 43
nutrition, xvi

Oatmeal Walnut Cookies, 102
Old Fashioned Oatmeal Cookies, 103
Orange Coconut Cake, 80
Orange Fruit Salad, 22
Orange Scones, 129
Orange-Scented Scones, 128
Orzo and Corn Off the Cob Salad, 19

pasta
  Barrett Family Macaroni and Cheese, 42
  Barrett Family Spaghetti and Meatballs, 37
  Carmola Quick Spaghetti, 36
  Healthy Chicken Salad, 31
  Homestyle Four-Cheese Macaroni, 42
  Johnny Brazili, 38
  Mom's Chicken Noodle Soup, 52
  Noodles and Broccoli with Saffron, 43
  Orzo and Corn off the Cob Salad, 19
  Robert's Lasagna, 38
  Three-Pepper Linguine, 44
Peach Delight, 115
Peach Delight with Pineapple, 116
Peach Mimosas, 123
Peach Praline Cobbler, 112
Peanut Butter Chocolate Chip Cookies, 104
Pecan Pie, 100
pecans
  Always Perfect Banana Bread, 126
  Apple Pound Cake, 78
  Big Mama's Apple Cake, 78
  Blue Cheese Ball, 6
  Bourbon Fudge, 118
  Butterscotch Brownies, 106
  Cranberry Relish, 68
  Italian Cream Cake, 87
  Joyce's Cranberry Salad, 20
  Lane Cake, 86
  Marcia Bernsten's English Toffee Cookies, 105
  Orange Scones, 145
  Peach Praline Cobbler, 112
  Pecan Pie, 100
  Rum Cake, 91
  Spicy Cheese Log, 6
  Strong Girl Brownies, 106
  Summit Lemon Squares, 107
  Sweet Pecans, 117
  Sweet Potato Casserole, 62
  Toffee or Pecan Pastries, 113
  Tossed Salad with Fruit and Nuts, 15
  Turtle Brownies, 107
Pepperoni Cheese Ball, 6
Persimmon Pudding, 111
Pineapple Casserole, 68
Pineapple Delight, 22
Pistachio Dessert, 116
Plantation Casserole, 34
Poppy Seed Salad Dressing, 24
pork
  Asparagus Rolls, 9
  Chopped South Carolina Barbecue, 33
  Down Home Ham and Potato Casserole, 34
  Eastern Carolina Barbecue, the Cheater's Version, 33
  Plantation Casserole, 34
  Rosemary Pork with Pears, 32
Potato Cheese Soup, 52
potatoes
  Down Home Ham and Potato Casserole, 34
  Garlic Rosemary Potatoes, 63

Gratin of Root Vegetables, 64
Low-Fat Potato Salad, 17
Potato Cheese Soup, 55
Red-Skin Potato Salad, 18
South of the Border Potato Salad, 18
potatoes, sweet
Gratin of Root Vegetables, 64
Roasted Sweet Potato Wedges, 62
Satia's Sweet Potato Pie, 99
Sweet Potato Casserole, 62
Sweet Potato Dumplings, 112
Sweet Potato Pie, 98
pumpkin
Grandmother Wheeless's Pumpkin Pie, 98
Jennifer's Favorite Pumpkin Pie, 96
Mrs. Williams's Pumpkin Pie, 97
Pumpkin Crisp Cake, 91
Pumpkin Crisp Cake, 91

Quiche Formula, 132
Quick and Easy Herb Bread, 75
Quick Coffee Cake, 130

Ranch Style Baked Beans, 65
Raspberry Vinaigrette, 16
Red-Skin Potato Salad, 18
Rich and Creamy Chocolate Frosting, 85
Roasted Beans with Garlic and Olives, 46
Roasted Sweet Potato Wedges, 62
Roasted Vegetables, 63
Robert's Ginger Cheesecake, 92
Robert's Lasagna, 38
Rosemary Pork with Pears, 32
Rum Cake, 91
Russian tea
Jennifer Huffingham's Russian Tea Mix, 121

salad dressings
Basic Vinaigrette, 15
Burgundy Bacon Vinaigrette, 24
Fennel Seed Vinaigrette, 23
French, 14
Poppy Seed, 24
Raspberry Vinaigrette, 16

Salmon Ball, 7
salsa
Black Bean Salsa, 23
sangria
Colombian Sangria, 123
Satia's Sweet Potato Pie, 99
Sausage Cheese Muffins, 132
seafood
Asian Salmon, 39
Georgia Shrimp Bake, 40
Salmon Ball, 7
Seven Seas Casserole, 41
Shrimp Jambalaya, 39
Spicy Tuna Croquettes, 41
Stir-Fried Shrimp and Snow Peas, 40
Tuna Chowder, 55
Sesame Cookies, 104
Seven Seas Casserole, 41
Seven-Layer Salad, 16
Seven-Minute Frosting, 81
Seven-Up® Pound Cake, 83
Shrimp Jambalaya, 39
Six-Minute Chocolate Cake, 84
sizes, standard, xv
slaw
Marinated Cabbage Slaw, 13
slow cookers
Best Ever Crock-Pot® Stew, 48
Chopped South Carolina Barbecue, 33
Eastern Carolina Barbecue, the Cheater's Version, 33
Five-Hour Stew, 49
Spicy Chili, 50
smoothies
Breakfast Smoothie, 131
Sock-It-To-Me Cake, 88
South of the Border Potato Salad, 18
Southern Corn Bread, 43
Southern Gingerbread and Lemon Sauce, 90
Spicy Cauliflower and Potatoes, 64
Spicy Cheese Log, 6
Spicy Chili, 50
Spicy Tuna Croquettes, 41
spinach
Joy White's Spinach Spread, 5
Spinach Artichoke Dip, 3

Spinach Tortilla Roll-Ups, 9
Very Berry Spinach Salad, 15
Spinach Artichoke Dip, 3
Spinach Tortilla Roll-Ups, 9
Squash and Cheese Casserole, 61
Squash Casserole, 61
Stir-Fried Shrimp and Snow Peas, 40
strawberries
Strawberry Cream, 117
Strawberry Pie, 95
Strawberry Shortcake, 88
Tossed Salad with Fruit and Nuts, 15
Very Berry Spinach Salad, 15
Strawberry Cream, 117
Strawberry Pie, 95
Strawberry Shortcake, 88
Strong Girl Brownies, 106
Stuffed Peppers, 45
Summit Lemon Squares, 107
Sweet and Sour Avocados, 10
Sweet and Sour Meatballs, 36
Sweet Pecans, 117
Sweet Potato Casserole, 62
Sweet Potato Dumplings, 112
Sweet Potato Pie, 98

Tabouleh, 67
Tender Dinner Knots, 75
Texas Chicken Loaf, 30
Three Sisters' Carrot Cake, 89
Three-Pepper Linguine, 44
Toffee or Pecan Pastries, 113
Toll House® Cake, 85
Tomato Pie, 61
Tossed Salad with Fruit and Nuts, 15
Tuna Chowder, 55
Turtle Brownies, 107
Twenty-Four-Hour Salad, 17
Twin City Housewife, The, xii

Vegetable Casserole, 60
Vegetarian Chili, Cincinnati-Style, 51
vegetarian entrees
Armenian Lentil Soup, 53
Barrett Family Macaroni and Cheese, 42
Curried Pea Soup, 54
Herbed Lentils and Rice, 44
Homestyle Four-Cheese Macaroni, 42
Noodles and Broccoli with Saffron, 43
Roasted Beans with Garlic and Olives, 46
Stuffed Peppers, 45
Three-Pepper Linguine, 44
Vegetarian Chili, Cincinnati-Style, 51
Very Berry Spinach Salad, 15
Virginia Spoon Bread, 71

Winston-Salem Journal, x, 13, 63, 84

Zucchini Bread, 127